Cari Donaldson

D0097032

Pope Awesome
and Other Stories

How I Found God, Had Kids,
and Lived to Tell the Tale

SOPHIA INSTITUTE PRESS
Manchester, New Hampshire

Sophia Institute Press
Box 5284, Manchester, NH 03108
1-800-888-9344

www.SophiaInstitute.com

Sophia Institute Press® is a registered trademark of Sophia Institute.

Library of Congress Cataloging-in-Publication Data
Donaldson, Cari.
    Pope awesome and other stories : how I found God, had kids, and lived to tell the tale / Cari Donaldson.
        pages cm
    ISBN 978-1-622821-56-3 (pbk. : alk. paper) 1. Donaldson, Cari. 2. Catholic converts—United States—Biography. I. Title.
    BX4668.D58A3 2013
    282.092—dc23
    [B]
                                                            2013031759

∞

Pope Awesome
and Other Stories

For Ken,
the kids,
and my guardian angel,
who have all, at some point,
saved my life

Contents

Author's Note

Gabriel, my five-year-old, pops his head into the kitchen.

"Gravity, Mommy," he says simply.

"*What's* gravity?" I ask, a little suspicious.

He sighs. "Gravity is a force that pulls objects to the center of the earth."

I stare at him. Why is he going on about gravity?

He explains a little more: "It also pulled all of Jude's toys out his window and into the pool."

"*What?*"

I jump up and run to the kitchen window. Sure enough, Gabriel's four-year-old brother, Jude, in protest against being sent to bed, has opened his bedroom window upstairs and flung every single toy from his room into the kiddie pool on the deck below.

Trying to control my temper, I decide to deal with the toys later and make this a teachable moment. "That was a good explanation of gravity, Gabriel. Can you tell me what letter *gravity* starts with?"

He looks at me blankly for a moment.

"Blue?"

This is our home. It's not the one we planned.

Pope Awesome and Other Stories

On August 6, 1999, my high school sweetheart and I were married in a twenty-minute Presbyterian ceremony that I insisted must be scrubbed clean of all references to Jesus. We were young and secular. We had a dual income and two dogs that stood in for the kids we swore we were never going to have.

It is now fourteen years, thousands of miles, and two conversions later. Not only are there kids—six of them—but they are kids with baptized, curious, and deep imaginations. They love Coke and sports and computer games, and they playact as knights, popes, princesses, superheroes, and saints.

Like their parents, they are firmly "in the world, but not of it." Like children, they embody perfect dignity and perfect comedy.

This book is about how our lives worked out differently from the way my husband and I planned, in every way.

And why.

—C.D.

∞

*Pope Awesome
and Other Stories*

Part 1

∞

Michigan

1

∞

In the Beginning

The world is a big place. Reading the news, it's easy to imagine that geography, politics, and selfishness divide us from each other so deeply that we can never be truly united to another person. And that God, if He is there, does not have the time or the energy to get involved with our lives. If you're someone with minimal religious devotion, these thoughts can swallow you whole.

But when you take the leap to look at the world through the eyes of faith, you start seeing God's fingerprints everywhere, creating connections so subtle, so delicate, they might pass unseen.

My husband, Ken, was born in Germany, in a military hospital on a U.S. Air Force base. His mother, a nineteen-year-old Texan, always said that in the Air Force, "even maternity wards are run like the military," with babies and mothers expected to follow strict schedules.

Three and a half years later and an ocean away, I was born in a civilian hospital outside Detroit, Michigan. By that time, Ken's father had left the air force, and his family of three began a long period of frequent moves, taking them to California, Nebraska, and Texas. Ken started the first grade four times in a single year.

While he was being taken on his tour of the West, I was growing up in Michigan, living in the same house where my mom had grown up. My childhood bedroom had been hers. Her kindergarten teacher still worked at my elementary school. Whereas Ken's family was like tumbleweed, never settling in one place for long, my family put down roots deeper than dandelions.

Then one day, the tumbleweeds boarded a plane, blew into Detroit Metro Airport, and touched down in Michigan. Ken's family moved into the same town I was growing up in, attended the same school system I was moving through, and became members of the same Presbyterian church I went to (like my mother before me). With a touch so light that nothing stirred in its wake, God brought Ken to me. I met him when I was thirteen. At fourteen, I knew I would marry him.

Ken's sister, Debra, was my age, and we got to know each other at school and at our church's youth group. That's where I first saw him.

October 15, 1989, marked our first date. I was a nervous freshman; Ken, a nervous senior. It was our high school's Homecoming Dance and my first date ever. I had spent weeks with my mom at stores, hunting down the perfect dress (an electric-blue, taffeta-and-black-velvet Jessica McClintock dress—*viva los '80s!*).

The date almost got derailed when, half an hour before Ken was due to arrive, my mom brought home a black kitten.

Mom and I had been trying to convince my dad that getting a cat would be a great idea, and *he* kept trying to convince *us* that it would be a spectacularly stupid one. We had been at that stalemate for a while when my mom, who was a visiting nurse, was offered the pick of the litter from a barn cat owned by one of her patients. Looking at the heap of cuteness there, Mom made her choice. On the way home, she called my dad and asked, "Would you divorce me if I brought a cat home?"

"What? *Divorce* you? No."

"Good. Because I'm bringing a cat home."

I meant to hold that bundle of black fuzz for only a moment, as I had a dance to primp for, but as I looked down at the kitten, plans changed.

"Why is the cat's fur *moving?*" I asked my mom. I was now holding the tiny animal far away from my body.

My mom peered closely at the kitten, while my dad stood in the kitchen doorway, making harrumphing noises. My mom and I came to the same realization at the same time.

Fleas.

This tiny kitten was so infested with fleas, you could see them *writhing* on its small body — in numbers so huge it made them clearly visible even against the cat's black fur.

We knew that if we surrendered to the horror and disgust that such a sight clearly warranted (All those fleas! In my *hands!*), my dad would banish the cat forever. Mom and I went into damage-control mode. She dug up a bottle of flea shampoo from the depths of the house, and I rolled up my sleeves and got elbow deep in lather and dying parasites.

By the time the kitty was sufficiently defleaed, I had only ten minutes to get ready for my date. Either out of a sincere desire to buy time for me or for the sake of sheer mischief, my younger brother, wearing a rubber Ronald Reagan mask, answered the door for Ken. While Ken stood in momentary confusion, I frantically toweled the remaining dead fleas off my arms, threw on my dress, and went out to meet my date.

And so our love affair was born.

Dramatics

It proved to be a torrid, on-again, off-again romance, made more hysterically dramatic by our age. The first time we broke up (*his* doing!) was only two months after our first date. As I numbly walked him to the door, my brain could only weakly think, "But I'm supposed to *marry* him," followed closely by, "I hope I left dirty Kleenex in the pocket of the letterman jacket he just asked me to give back."

Despite all indications to the contrary, my broken heart didn't kill me. Life went on as if it honestly couldn't care less about a failed high school romance. My freshman year ended, Ken graduated and went to college, and a huge geographical distance opened between us once again.

I kept going to church and its youth group, because that's what you did where I grew up. You went to church on Sunday. During the service, you read from your gold-foil-covered *Good News Bible* with the crinkly, onion-skin paper and odd little stick-figure illustrations, and then went to the fellowship hall to eat a square of coffeecake and drink a cup of punch.

The rest of the week, you kept God under wraps. My Midwestern, middle-class upbringing left religion more or less a private pursuit, with outward displays of faith to be avoided, except for grace before Thanksgiving dinner. Even the youth group was focused on "practical skills" like team-building and "What would you do in this moral dilemma?" rather than on faith formation.

But from a very early age, I remember talking to God. Every night, I imagined sharing a telephone connection with Him. When I had exhausted that day's topics with Him, I'd ask Him to "put my Grandpa on." I'd wait while God looked through the rooms of Heaven, hunting down my Grandpa Bob, who had died when I was five. Once God had found him and handed him the prayer phone, Grandpa and I would chat a bit; then I'd give my love to him and to God and drift off to sleep.

Beyond that, religion was just a pretty background for my life, a way to mark the passing of the year. That's how, at the Christmas Eve service a year after our initial breakup, Ken came home from college, went to church with his family, saw me there with *my* family, and realized he missed me. (I credit my Christmas dress for this.) We got back together. I was happy to let the rest of my high school years pass, swept up in the tidal wave of first love.

My rather unformed and uninformed prayer life continued as before. Which may be why, when a friend lent me a copy of a particular anti-Christian book the summer before I left for college, I was fertile ground for its message.

The book, a work of historical fiction, strove to strip Jesus, and by extension, Christianity, of anything divine or mystical. It had footnotes galore, and to a seventeen-year-old girl with little grounding in theology, it was a revelation.[1] I had no education in Christian apologetics to help me critically assess the book, so I was happy to embrace the whole anti-Christian concept. The ability to toss aside some Bronze-Age set of patriarchal ethics while spouting quotes from a historical novel feels very grown up to a new college student. So, convinced that at its heart, Christianity was nothing more than a monstrous tale of a monstrous God who sacrificed His Son to Himself to appease His own anger, I chucked it all.

More or less. I still retained a prayer life, and through that tenuous connection, the desire to know my Creator—to really *know* Him—was never far from my heart. I refused to look for

---

[1] See? Aren't these things impressive?

Him in Christianity, but my soul would keep scanning the landscape, searching for Him the way you scan a crowd, searching for a familiar face.

Ken and I would break up and then reconcile, break up and then reconcile, with each breakup cycle featuring greater theatrics. Once I took all the letters and poems he had written me over the past four years and burned them in the parking lot of my dorm.

As a result of another breakup I cut my hair in a do-it-yourself project that went horribly wrong. My roommate had been away that weekend. When she opened the door to our dorm room and saw my coiffure, she wearily sighed, "What did Ken do this time?"

Eventually Ken and I went up in flames — ignited by a fight over a missed exit on the highway. I figured I had heard the last of him. Who stays with a high school sweetheart, anyway?

My breakup with God was less dramatic, but no less painful. He and I went what I thought were our separate ways when I figured four years of drinking and card games were more interesting than classes or responsibility. I stopped going to church and started reading all the New Age, occult materials I could get my hands on. Occasionally, I went to classes, did poorly, and mostly drifted from one weekend to the next, looking to drink and play euchre.

As far as I was concerned, neither God nor Ken deserved me.

About Euchre

Anyone who is or is friends with a Michigander already knows what euchre is. If you don't personally know a Michigander, I offer my sincere apologies, and urge you to set down this book and run — *run!* — to the nearest auto show or hockey game. In either place, you're sure to find a Michigander who can teach you.

Briefly, euchre is a card game that uses just the cards from nine up. Four people play, in teams of two. The jack is high, each player is dealt five cards, and through a series of "tricks," teams play until someone has scored ten points. I won't go into further detail for you, since I can see your eyes glazing over.[2]

The thing about euchre is that, much like playground games, while the general rules are the same from place to place, each individual house comes up with its own variations, such as Screw the Dealer, Aces No Faces, Farmer's Hand, and so on.

You can tell a lot about someone by the modifications she makes to the game. When I was in college, I made all of them. I did everything I could to make my euchre hand as easy and as stacked in my own favor as possible. I didn't want to think. I didn't want to struggle. I certainly didn't want to lose. I just wanted to drink whatever someone had illegally bought for my underage group of friends and play euchre in my dorm room until the cards grew gray from use.

Since the game uses a short deck and requires you to keep track of only five cards, it's easy enough to play when you're less than sober. Which is to say that Michiganders don't play with a full deck. There are lots of metaphors you can draw from euchre.

Reconciled

For the rest of my life, I will be indebted to my sister-in-law, Debra. If she and I ever find ourselves stranded on a desert

---

[2] Unless you're a Michigander, in which case you're probably scanning the room for three other people to get up a quick game.

island together, I will think it my absolute duty to will myself dead, just so she has a protein source to sustain her life. Why? For the simple fact that her scheming and duplicity ended the last estrangement that Ken and I would ever have to endure.

Because Debra and I had been friends even before I had met her brother, we kept in touch. I opened my e-mail one day during my senior year and was pleasantly surprised to see a message from her. I had managed to curb my drinking and euchre-playing just enough to pull my grades out of the gutter, apply to the university's education-degree program in a fit of "what am I going to do with my life after graduation?" and was beyond shocked to find that I had been accepted. And while I was still far, far away from God and Ken, there was still a large, loud part of me that wanted to be close to both of them again.

As I scanned Debra's e-mail, I grew confused and puzzled. She said Ken had been asking about me. She talked about how he had pressed her to ask me if I would possibly consider sending him an e-mail, just to catch up.

"Catch up"? We hadn't spoken in over two years, and it seemed clear to me that we were just supposed to move on with these lives apart. It felt as if the words were acid, shot right into my brain. I couldn't think.

I did ultimately e-mail him—sending a taunting, mean-spirited message. He responded with complete sincerity, genuine happiness that I had e-mailed him. I was taken off guard by my own feelings of remorse for my cruelty. We haltingly set up arrangements for him to come visit me at college one day, to go out to dinner.

I told myself I felt sorry for him—sorry that he missed me so much that he was willing to go through sisterly channels. But the truth was that there was always a part of me waiting for him, looking for him out of the corner of my eye. Debra's e-mail was just a convenient excuse. Years later, she confessed to me the depths of her deviousness. While Debra was e-mailing me, insisting that Ken was wondering if I'd e-mail him, she was concurrently e-mailing her brother, telling *him* that I had approached *her*, asking for his e-mail address, to drop him a line.

We were gullible victims of the crisscross, the oldest trick in the book.

Our first dinner was hours and hours long. We sat in a local pizza joint, surrounded by the stoned and rowdy weekend crowd. The noise level of the clientele required that we lean in toward each other, bending across the table to hear each other speak.

One dinner led to another. Then another. Then one night, we were back in my apartment, talking idly before he got back into his car and made the hour trip back to Detroit. He was sitting in a chair my grandmother had made me, and I was on the floor at his side. Without being entirely aware of what was coming out of my mouth, I found myself telling him how much I had missed him. How much these meetings had meant to me. How much I didn't want them to end. I felt as if I were swimming through honey. He kept smiling at me. They were huge smiles that broke his whole face in two—and which told me that he couldn't remember the last time he had smiled.

So there, in a dingy Lansing apartment, the night of August 31, 1997, while the rest of the world watched tragedy unfold in a Paris tunnel, Ken and I were reconciled, the grateful victims of his sister's manipulations.[3]

---

[3] Other historical date coincidences: Our first breakup was on Pearl Harbor Day. The first time we got back together, the

Pope Awesome and Other Stories

Two Semesters and a Wedding

Despite all my attempts to make my college years a wasteland, I graduated and landed a job immediately. I found myself teaching English and social studies to middle schoolers, in the same district I had graduated from. I was living with my parents. Some of my new colleagues, in fact, were parents of childhood friends.

I was shocked to discover that I really enjoyed middle schoolers. I liked their gangling awkwardness; I liked their floundering between childhood and adulthood. I liked their questioning of everything. It doesn't take a psychologist to reveal that I saw myself in their growing pains. While I *now* see God's hand in the decisions of my life *then*, old me didn't notice Him standing right next to me.

Old me did, however, notice Ken—specifically, that despite our glorious reunification, the relationship was not advancing where I thought it should go as quickly as I thought it should. I had known we were going to get married for the past eight years—since I was fourteen. The fact that he didn't seem to realize that it was time to pop the question was mystifying.

Every time I pressed the issue, it came down to finances. He was working for a parts supplier—a warehouse job that, despite wages that were not horrible, wasn't exactly an up-and-coming position. But after an eternity of a few months, during which I contributed a bit to the cost of a ring, since I was paying no

---

Berlin Wall fell within twenty-four hours. Our final reconciliation was the night Lady Di died, and through no fault of our own, we were married on the fifty-fourth anniversary of the bombing of Hiroshima. We claim no responsibility for any of the events.

rent, he got onto his knees and proposed to me. The details are lost in a surreal haze. But the next thing I knew, I had a $500 ring on my finger, finally engaged to be married to Ken. That night at dinner, we showed it off to his father, who was in town on a business trip.

We knew we didn't want to be married by a justice of the peace, although neither of us could articulate why not. We weren't attending any church at the time, and I was still clinging to a college-era set of New Agey philosophies. When my mom suggested Ken and I contact the pastor of our childhood church, it seemed as good an idea as any.

We met with the pastor. He gave us a set of common wedding vows and told us to come up with something that suited our taste. I took him at his word and proceeded to cut and paste a line from this version into a phrase from that version, taking this paragraph but not that one, and everywhere—*everywhere*—I made sure to cut out the name of Jesus. I would be married in a church, but you couldn't get me to allow Jesus' name to be uttered in it.

At some point during the wedding preparations, one of my students approached me after class. He had a paper in his hand, and he put it down on my desk in front of me.

"Would you be my sponsor?" he said, pushing the paper closer to me.

"Your what?" I asked, glancing at the paper and seeing that the name of the local Catholic Church was on the letterhead.

"My sponsor. For Confirmation. I need an adult." Students started trickling in for the next class. The boy shifted in agitation. I could tell he didn't want to do this with an audience.

"Confirmation?" I felt as if I were suddenly robbed of my ability to speak English. What was this boy talking about? Why was he still in my class? Didn't he know he was going to be tardy?

"Yeah. Confirmation." At this point, his eyebrow started wrinkling, as if he was seriously wishing he could hit the rewind button on the last two minutes of his life.

"Do ... do you have to be Catholic to be a sponsor?" I asked. He nodded, carefully, as you would to a very small child.

"I'm not Catholic," I said. He drew back and blinked at me in disbelief. We'd now drawn a small crowd, and although I tried to shoo the other students to their seats, they hovered around us.

"You're not?" the boy asked, incredulously. I shook my head. "Really? What are you then?"

I spread my hands out and mumbled something noncommittal. He took the paper with him and left for his next class right as the late bell rang.

I don't know whom he got to be his sponsor.

His question stayed with me. What *was* I? I knew what I *wasn't*. I wasn't a Presbyterian, despite the fact that I was soon to be married in one of their churches. I wasn't even Christian, since I made sure Jesus got snubbed from the guest list. The hodgepodge of occult and New Age ideas I had gleefully piled around me during college were quickly growing tedious in their lack of substance. I wanted God. I wanted to be close to Him, or Her, or It, or whatever that entity was that I found myself praying to, night after night. I longed for God's presence the same way I had longed for Ken's when we were broken up. But wherever I looked for His presence, there was only enough of it there to make me realize how much I wanted it.

"Later," I told myself. Later, I'd get to the bottom of this "God" thing. First I had a wedding to plan and execute.

In the Beginning

On August 6, 1999, almost ten years after our first date, Ken and I stood in front of a crowd of friends and family and made our vows to each other. And while I thought I had made it clear He wasn't welcome, Jesus was there too, joining man and woman into one.

The Only House I Ever Hunted

A year after the wedding, we found ourselves in a position to make a modest down payment on a house. We couldn't afford to live in the school district I taught in, so we turned our eye closer to Detroit. There, in a quiet neighborhood populated by old couples who had moved in fifty years before, thanks to the GI Bill, we found our home.

Our neighbors were wonderful. On one side was a couple who spent winters in Florida. The back neighbors were Lebanese immigrants who every year tried to coax their quince tree into bloom. To the right was an ancient couple and their fifty-something unmarried son. He kept the most amazing garden in the backyard—and was the groundskeeper for St. Sabina Catholic Church, one block away.

St. Sabina.[4] We could hear its bells every day, and I'd pause what I was doing to listen. On Sundays you could see people leaving their houses and walking to church, patting the feet of the statue that even I could recognize as the Virgin Mary. "Such affection for a stone," I'd snort. I would shake my head at the superstition of fools and go back to what I was doing.

And there was always so much to be done. The house was in desperate need of care; the lady who had lived there last was an

---

[4] Catholic convert and martyr. Her accuser and executioner bore the curious name of Elpidio the Perfect. Apparently, he wasn't.

elderly shut-in, an enthusiastic smoker. Tar covered every inch of the house. We Kilzed all the walls, then decided on colors. There were two obvious bedrooms and a third that had been used as a dining room, so that's how we kept it. We chose the larger, shoebox-size bedroom for ourselves.

Even before we got married, Ken had said he didn't want children. Despite the fact that kids loved him, he was adamant. I was ambivalent, so his firm opinion outweighed my lack of one. There was no need to wonder if we should turn that last bedroom into a nursery. We would remain blissfully child-free. We acquired two rescued greyhounds and told both our mothers that these were the only grandbabies they could expect from us.

That Nagging Feeling

Summers were weird for me. While I loved, absolutely loved, having them off, I was never quite sure what to do with my time. In college, I took classes year-round and worked several jobs in between, and even the last years of high school found me with a summer job, so this swath of free time was something new. I'd walk the dogs, paint, or make something for the house, but eventually a restlessness I associated with boredom would return.

Having hours to fill meant that I soon found myself pondering God again. "What if …" I wondered. What if this restlessness *wasn't* boredom? What if it was my looking for God? I hadn't found Him in the tailor-made religion I had crafted for myself in college, so what about an organized religion? What about a religion that had already hammered out the Big Questions and had the staying power and followers to prove it?

Anything had to be better than the gnawing, howling emptiness in me. So I started a systematic recon mission on all the world's great religions. There was only one caveat: the religion couldn't ask me to worship a created thing.

That was the only enduring lesson I had learned during my stint immersed in New Age theology. To give your worship—defined as a focus and admiration you give to no other thing—to a created object was folly. Why worship Athena if her father, Zeus, was strong enough to create her? It would be like worshipping a painting and ignoring the hand that painted it. I wanted a relationship with the Creator of all things. To stop the search at a created object would be to end the search prematurely.

Under this beam of insight, all the pagan pantheons of my New Age period crumbled. Trace any pagan deity back far enough and you're left with a personification of the earth. Even I wasn't dumb enough to think that this planet was the creator of all life throughout the cosmos.

I stared with Buddhism, since at the time I still believed in the theory of reincarnation. It was friendly territory.

However, it was immediately obvious that Buddhism was more of a philosophical system. In the theology department, it ranged from noncommittal agnosticism to flat-out atheism. Since the existence of God had never been an issue for me, but rather, God's nature and the best way to develop a relationship with it, I quickly turned away and set my sights on Hinduism, another reincarnation-friendly theology.

Hinduism didn't last long, either. I quickly learned that the pantheon was another created god after created god. That, coupled with its nebulous, unknown beginnings, meant you could never trace the religion back to its original source to see how it was meant to be practiced from its beginning. Judaism had Moses and the Torah, Christianity had Jesus and the Bible, Islam had Muhammad and the Koran, all of which could help illustrate the original intentions of the belief system, but Hinduism had none of this. There was no known founder, no original set of instructions, just generations of oral tradition. With those things absent, how could you ever be sure that what you were doing was the way God intended you to worship Him? It wasn't for me.

Next I explored Islam, but I ran up against problems from the beginning. The biggest one was the concept that unless one was reading the Koran in its original Arabic, there was no way of knowing that you had an accurate translation. My inability to learn Arabic, coupled with the serious shortcoming of a religion unable to come up with a central authority to translate its holy texts faithfully meant that Islam was shelved rather quickly.

Judaism was next. But besides the obvious fact that the form of Judaism practiced in the Bible didn't exist anymore, it felt too close to Christianity. It was like declaring your independence from your parents, but going to live rent free with your grandfather. I spent time reading the Old Testament and feeling more and more resentful about the whole search. I felt very sorry for the human condition in general and myself in particular. Poor humanity—to be burdened with the desire to know a God who seemed to delight in hiding from them.

Despite an entire summer spent in agonized search for God, I was no closer than I was three months before. As far as I was concerned, I had exhausted all the options, and I was still left floundering on my own.

I experienced an atypical depression around this time. I'd mope around the house for days, and when asked about my behavior, I'd launch into some sermon about how God kept running away from me, no matter how hard I tried to hunt Him down.

In the Beginning

One day, exasperated with my existential whining, Ken irritably said, "Why don't you just pick something to believe in and believe in it?"

That stopped me in my tracks. For one thing, Ken never got upset about my spiritual questing, so for him to be annoyed meant that I had crossed a line somewhere. The other thing that hit home for me was the very nature of the question. What was wrong with me? Why couldn't I just pick something that fit with my worldview and settle in there? Why did I have to make everything so darn *complicated*? Surely there were enough people in my acquaintance who insisted that all one needed to do in life was be a good person and that would be enough. Why couldn't I just do that?

That was the kick in the pants I needed to convince me that something beyond myself was spurring this search. Left to my own devices, I would have kicked the whole God question to the curb and followed a path that offered maximum good feelings with minimum work on my part. But I had tried that, and it didn't work. It didn't make the gnawing sense of something missing go away. So as much as I wanted to chuck the whole thing, Ken's words made me realize that there was no rest for the wicked, and I couldn't stop this search until I found truth.

2

∞

Rugrats

Ken's thirtieth birthday was on an early-spring day of freak beauty. In late March there was snow on the ground in Michigan more often than not, but that year we were spared. On our way to dinner at an Italian restaurant, I was uncharacteristically behind the wheel, and was feeling very happy and optimistic. The sun was out, the snow was gone, and if you looked closely enough, you could imagine you saw buds on the forsythia bushes.

The highway exit was a long, wide arc around a marshy area. It reminded me of a roller-coaster track.

"A couple of rugrats wouldn't be so bad," Ken said.

Just like that. Apropos of absolutely *nothing*. My stomach dropped — just as it does on roller-coaster rides. We hadn't been talking about children. We hadn't even been *talking*. We had just been driving to dinner, happily enjoying each other's company in silence and the sunshine. And now he goes and turns my whole world upside down with a single, careless sentence?

I stared at him briefly, then put my eyes back on the road. I said nothing. He said nothing further. I got us to the restaurant in once piece, and we ate dinner. If he noticed the giant, rugrat-shaped elephant of his own creation at the table with us, he didn't let on.

I tried to chalk up Ken's comment as a momentary lapse into psychosis brought on by some vague brooding on his mortality triggered by his thirtieth birthday. That's all it was. He had certainly never given any other indication that he was harboring a desire for children, so it seemed as if I could put the whole thing out of my mind.

Which might have been easier to do, had my daily commute not taken me past the exit where the Rugrat Comment was made. Ten times a week I passed that spot, and each time I did, it was as if a billboard had been erected there—THIS IS WHERE KEN SAID HE WANTED KIDS. RIGHT HERE. KIDS.

We had made our decision about this already. As long as I had known Ken, I had known he didn't want children. I was ambivalent about them, so his desire to remain childless didn't bother me. I had never been around many babies growing up. My only sibling was only two years younger, so I had no memories of him as a baby. I didn't babysit much in high school. None of my friends had infant brothers or sisters. Babies were pretty much an abstract concept that other people dealt with. We had informed the mothers-in-law. We rescued two greyhounds, and those were our children. Dual income, no kids, the planet's already overpopulated anyway, so we're doing it a favor, really.

For the next three months, though, every time I passed that spot on the highway, I wondered. Then summer vacation came, and I didn't have to take that route to work, and thoughts of children faded to the background, eclipsed by my spiritual crisis and obsessive study of world religion.

It was one of the final weeks of vacation when I got a call from a friend I had known since grade school. She wanted to get together for lunch. Did I want to meet her three-month-old son?

Rugrats

Honestly, I wasn't sure. I mean, I loved her, and I loved her husband—whom I had known since high school. But their infant son? That seemed so ... *parental.*

But since I had nothing else to fill the time slot, I agreed. The first infant in who-knows-how-long would be admitted into my brick ranch domicile.

I was a goner as soon as I saw him. He was bald and fat and had these huge blue eyes, and he was so, so adorable. It was painful how cute he was. My friend laid him on the floor while we chatted, and I kept staring at this tiny-but-not-tiny human being that two people I had grown up with had created. I kept staring at my friend, trying to wrap my head around the fact that she was now a *mother.* I had known her since third grade—I had flown kites with her. I had had sleepovers with her. I had been to see Prince in concert with her. And now here she was, sitting on the floor next to her *son.* A mom.

The three of us went to lunch, and I was shocked by how not weird it seemed. I'm not sure what I had been expecting, but I hadn't imagined that going out in public with a little human would feel so normal.

Then the baby started to cry. Loudly. I passed him back to his mom and tried to offer every bit of useless help I could. Did he need a pacifier? A blanket? Milk? What could I do to help him?

All of the sudden, I realized that I wasn't trying to get him to stop crying because we were in the middle of a restaurant and, oh my gosh, everyone else's lunch would be absolutely ruined if they had to endure a single minute of unhappy baby sounds.

No. I was trying to get him to stop crying because he was sad. There was something wrong with his little baby world, and I wanted to make it better. Two hours with this child, and I already loved him.

It was the first time I had thought of a child in terms of his needs and not my own. One meal with a baby, and I found myself pulled—completely unexpectedly—a tiny way out of myself. I glanced at my friend again, who was eating lunch with one hand and nursing the now-happy baby with the other. She looked like some casual, effortless supermom. I wondered what it was like to live inside her head, to feel constantly the love and concern of which I had just felt a tiny flicker. I wondered if she could feel her motherhood, settled around her shoulders like a coat.

Ken came home from work that day to find me on the bed, sobbing. I was sprawled out, face down, and I had left teary, snotty trails on the green velvet of our comforter. Alarmed, he asked me what was wrong. Was I hurt? Had someone died? What was going on?

I rolled over and looked up at him, miserably. "I want kids. I just realized that I want a baby, and I know you don't, and this is the sort of thing that you're supposed to hammer out before you get married because this is the sort of thing that breaks up marriages and we'd already hammered it out but now I've changed my mind and I'm scared this is going to make us get a divorce."

I let it all out in a single sobbing, hysterical breath, before I lost my nerve and wasn't brave enough to admit this to my husband. He sat next to me on the bed, looking at the wall. For a long moment, he didn't say anything, just letting me cry some more.

Then he turned to look at me, and said, "Nothing is going to break up our marriage. Nothing. And you don't have to worry about a baby."

He stood up and left the room. I wasn't entirely certain what he had meant, but I found hope stirring in my heart.

Rugrats

Congratulations on All Your Endeavors

Much as the specific words that Ken chose to propose to me are lost to history, the actual point where we decided to try to conceive a child is hazy to me. Now I can look back and see the progression from Ken's "rugrat" bombshell, to my hysterical confession that I wanted kids, to an actual decision to have them as being something soaked in grace and guided by Providence. But at the time, it was mostly a jumble of crazy.

Being thoroughly clueless on the subject, we decided that it would be best if the baby were born as close to the start of my summer vacation as possible. That way, I wouldn't have to take any time off work, and by the time school started again in September, the baby would be old enough to go to daycare.

So, having completely bought the culture's lie that children are a consumable good, existing for the pleasure of adults, we planned to get pregnant in October, with a July due date. We'd squeeze a pregnancy into our timetable, so as to not be inconvenienced too much. The thought that we might have problems conceiving, or, at the very least, not get pregnant the first time we tried, never crossed our arrogant minds. We wanted a child, and we wanted it born in the summer.

I started gathering intel on this conception thing as if I were planning a field trip. What arrangements needed to be made? What were the possible road bumps we could encounter? How much time did we need? I bought prenatal vitamins, ovulation predictor kits, and for the first time in my life, I started charting my cycles. I pinpointed the optimal window on the calendar—and that's where the first wrench was thrown into my plans.

Every October, Ken and his dad went fishing in northern Michigan. His mom would come too, and while the men spent whole days getting soaked in freezing water and handling massive, and massively stinky, fish, she and I would stay at my house enjoying the comforts of not-a-fishing-camp. Usually, the fishing trip was a week long, but this year Ken was going to cut it short for a Very Special Reason.

I had already spilled the reason to my mom and was planning on sharing it with my mother-in-law over dinner during her stay.

We were at a local Mexican restaurant, a couple of margaritas in, when my mother-in-law started telling a story about a recent outing she had taken, where she came across some heirloom baby spoons. Holding them in her hands, she started to cry, realizing that she had never had a reason to buy something like that. I pushed her margarita closer to her.

"You have a reason now!" I blurted out. "Ken and I have decided we're going to have a baby!" She stared at me blankly for a moment.

"You *what?*... When?"

"Now!" I yelled, making a sweeping gesture with my glass and sloshing some drink out in the process. "Well, in a couple days, anyway. Ken's coming home early from the fishing trip because *now's the time!*"

If there is a more elegant way to explain to your mother-in-law that you're going to need the house to yourself for a couple of hours, I don't know what it is. Ken cut his trip short and came home. My father-in-law, unaware of the change in child plans, had opted to finish out the week at the cabin, and my mother-in-law made plans to have dinner with friends that night. She came back much later with a card for us.

On the front was a picture of fireworks. On the inside, it said, "Congratulations on all your endeavors."

Rugrats

The motto "God loves a fool" should be on my family crest, for it certainly sums up this chapter of my life. Sure enough, our first child was conceived on our time schedule, thus unlocking a secret storehouse of crazy that I didn't know existed inside me. Imagine all the insane things first-time mothers do—compounded with the fact that I was still in the throes of spiritual turmoil—and you have someone who was hysterically, obsessively concerned with engineering the perfect environment to grow her child's body *and* soul.

Not only did I avoid the usual suspects—alcohol, caffeine, and deli meats—I also found a whole new level of potential hazards to make myself crazy with: nail polish (chemicals could leach into my bloodstream and poison the baby!), anything that so much as touched plastic (hormone disrupters!), and all water that might have once passed through lead pipes (I lived in a house built in 1951. Everything around me was lead based).

As for the spiritual development of my tiny child, I was just as annoying. Any form of entertainment that included anything violent or angry was to be avoided, lest the negativity seep into the baby's tiny soul. This meant, of course, that the majority of radio fare was out, and I spent the entire school year driving in to work listening only to the soundtrack from "O! Brother, Where Art Thou?" and Tori Amos CDs.

However, my deeply capricious nature still shone through. I had no problem eating caffeine-laden chocolate like it was going out of style, or playing the Diablo computer game—which is violent *and* rife with demonic imagery—with Ken every night. When you're making it all up as you go along, you have no problem with inconsistencies like these.

Slowly, so, so slowly, the months passed. I thought I had everything ready. The gender-neutral clothes had all been washed in Dreft, folded, and stacked neatly in the nursery next to the Diaper Genie refills. The books had been read and reread. A collection of soothing birth music had been compiled and burned onto a CD. The end of the school year had come and gone, so I had a long summer vacation ahead of me—one I couldn't wait to share with our child.

Ken and I went to grab dinner at Red Robin, and halfway through the meal, I felt a horrible pain. Worse than round-ligament pain. Worse than the increasingly irritating Braxton-Hicks ("false labor") contractions.

I stood up. Ken looked at me oddly. I sat down. The pain went away.

We went home. We started watching the exciting series finale of *Bachelorettes in Alaska*, and an odd sensation started spreading across my abdomen. It didn't hurt; it was just annoying. It wouldn't go away, so I figured I'd call my mother-in-law to see what she thought.

In the days before this, my dad had convinced my mom to go on a quick weekend camping trip, swearing on a stack of Bibles that he'd bought a signal booster for the cell phone, so I would be able to reach them if I went into labor. Reluctantly, my mom agreed, but so reluctantly that I didn't want to bother her by calling to report this new, ridiculous, probably nothing development.

Instead, I described the symptoms to my mother-in-law, who was 750 miles away in Georgia. She agreed that it sounded promising, and it might be the start of labor. If it was, she advised, it would be wise to get as much rest as possible now, before there was no more rest to be had.

We went to bed. But of course we were too revved up to sleep.

Rugrats

I tossed and turned. The contractions, although still not painful, wouldn't go away. We got up and hung out in the midnight darkness of our backyard. I was restless and cagey. We walked around the block. The contractions were regular and started to get an edge to them. We went back inside.

I was struck by the realization that this was our last night together of just the two of us. By tomorrow, everything would be changed forever, and even if we were ninety, and once again in a house devoid of children, we'd never go back to how it was right now. This man, whom I had known and loved since I was a child, was about to have a child of his own that he could hold and kiss and father.

The next contraction was too painful for me to dwell on that last thought. We figured it was probably time to start calling people, even though it was very, very early morning. My mom would never forgive anyone if she missed the birth of her firstborn grandchild.

I called her cell phone. It went straight to voicemail.

I panicked.

I tried again. Still voicemail. My dad's signal booster wasn't working! My parents were three and a half hours away—who knew how long a labor could last? Ken suggested we call my brother and see if he'd be willing to take a one-o'clock-in-the-morning jaunt up to Gaylord to fetch my parents from their camper.

My brother was called. My brother sensibly suggested calling the campground office first. If that failed, perhaps the local sheriff's department could help out. He also generously offered to make the calls himself, since clearly Ken and I had entered "first-time parent psychosis" and couldn't problem-solve our way out of a paper bag.

I got up to go to the bathroom and was overcome with a contraction so painful that I told Ken it was time to go. I didn't plan on getting an epidural, but I figured the pain would make more sense in a hospital.

We got in the car and drove our way over streets riddled with potholes. We got to the hospital around 2 a.m., I was put into some sort of triage room, where I was given a cervical exam and was told I was only two centimeters dilated and they were going to send me home.

Send me home? What? None of this was part of the plan. See? Here's our birth plan right here. Soothing music and no pain meds unless asked for. Nothing about being sent home once we got here.

The nurse told me I wasn't in active labor, and unless my water had broken, I couldn't stay. While she said this, she was testing to see if there was any sign of amniotic fluid.

There was.

Now the story was different. She demanded to know when my water had broken, and why hadn't I told them this earlier?

I told her I had no idea that my water had broken, and maybe it really hadn't, but if it would help me stay, I'd happily make up a time when my water had broken.

The nurse wasn't amused.

While this was playing out, my brother had managed to get hold of someone at the campground, who then went over to my parents' campsite and knocked on the door. A knock on the door of your camper in the middle of the night when your daughter is set to have her baby any day doesn't need an explanation. While my dad thanked the messenger, my mom frantically tried to get a signal on the cell phone, slowly circling the campsite, jabbing the phone skyward, willing it to get reception.

Rugrats

They dressed, jumped into the car, and headed back to Detroit. By the time they met up with my brother and got to the hospital, I was in an actual room and was still not progressing.

That's when the walking began.

We walked the maternity ward. And walked. And walked. And walked. Between boredom and pain, I have only flashes of memories of this time, but everyone there assures me that we walked for hours.

At some point, the pain got the better of me. I wanted a shot of Stadol. I wanted it *now*. I made this demand very clear to husband, mother, father, brother, nurses, and a random visitor to the maternity wing, but nothing happened. No pain meds came.

Back in bed, I asked Ken why no one had given me the drugs. He looked at me curiously. He informed me that I hadn't told anyone that I needed them. And no, telepathic requests didn't count. I had to actually speak.

Clearly, everyone was insane.

Ken conveyed my request to the nurse, who then (unfairly) made me sit on a fetal monitor for a million years before I got the drugs.

Slooooooowly, I dilated. So. Freaking. Slowly.

Finally, I felt that urge to push that is more irresistible than love, more consuming than hunger. I had to push, and push I was going to do. I made sure to verbalize this intention to Ken, who relayed it to the nurse.

She checked me. Still not ten centimeters, no pushing yet.

Over the course of the next several contractions, Ken was tasked with the thankless job of trying to get me not to push. He urged me to remember the proper breathing for this situation. I ignored him. He told me not to squish up my face, because he suspected that meant I was trying to sneak in some pushes.

The only time I got even slightly surly with anyone was at that moment. "I'll squish my face if I want to squish my face!" I informed him forcefully.

The nurse checked me again. Time to push (duh—that's what I'd been telling you lunatics). My mom, dad, and brother left, a riot of activity immediately swirled around me, and despite all the people suddenly in the room, I was faced with this task that only I could do. No matter how much support and love I was surrounded with, I was the only person in the world who could help this child enter the world.

I pushed. I marveled at the immediate absence of pain. It was completely gone, and I wondered briefly why that glorious development wasn't ever covered in childbirth classes.

I pushed. A head emerged. The doctor encouraged me to reach down and feel my baby's head. I declined. Who wants to pause to fiddle about with a head when I can have the whole baby in a few more pushes?

The doctor's voice, amused and startled, "The baby! It just bit me!"

Another push.

And Lotus made her entrance into the world.

I asked all the delirious, weary-frantic questions new mothers ask: "Is she ok? Why isn't she crying? Why *is* she crying? What are they doing? I want my baby. No, seriously, why won't they give me my dang baby?"

She was placed into my arms, crying these amazing goat-like cries, her little bottom lip quivering.

She was perfect. She was nothing like I had imagined, because my imagination was too small to ever dream up something as sublime as she was. She was like touching eternity and being able to hold it in my arms.

Rugrats

I Have Called You by Your Name

We named her Isabella Lotus. The naming process was arduous, and it was ultimately a trap I had set for Ken. We had bought a painfully hipster book of names,[5] which we had pored over with no agreed-upon name in sight. I was gunning for a Lotus. It may have been nothing more than a hangover from my New Age years, but I was convinced that the lotus flower was a striking image for the human spiritual experience. Born in the muck and the dark of pond silt, the lotus senses and seeks out the sun, growing ever upward, until it breaks through the water's surface and bursts into the most glorious of flowers. I was still wallowing around somewhere between muck and sunlight, but I was going to give my daughter every leg up I could—starting with her name.

But no matter how many times I suggested it for our possible daughter, Ken refused. Ultimately, I had to be satisfied with his agreeing to let me have it as a middle name, although I knew that I was going to call her Lotus, and only Lotus, as long as she would let me. We settled on the "little princess"[6] name of Isabella as a first name, and so our firstborn child came into the world, as Isabella Lotus Donaldson.[7]

It didn't take long for the postpartum, babymoon, oh-my-gosh-we're-parents phase to end and for me to turn my thoughts once again to matters spiritual. The subject of baptism kept

---

[5] The book came complete with its own name-rating system: a "PB&J name" was a dull, safe name, a "pocket T name" was a classic, like a white pocket T-shirt, a "little princess" name was self-explanatory, a "map name" charted the curious trend of naming children after geographical locations, etc., etc.

[6] According to our hipster baby-name book.

[7] If she had been a boy: Ewan Michael Donaldson.

bubbling to the surface of my mind, kind of like a lotus rising toward the sun, and I grew increasingly desperate to find a way to reconcile such an embarrassingly Christian concept with my noncommittal belief system.

Finally, I hit upon it. I vaguely remembered a story about my aunt and uncle baptizing their oldest daughter when she was a baby. My uncle had written something about my newborn cousin being a "child of the universe," and that phrase clicked with me. Regardless of what he meant when he wrote it, I would comfortably personify "the Universe" as a sort of God stand-in. I got a copy of the poem from my aunt, asked my cousin (the "child of the universe" in question) to be Lotus's godmother, I rounded up any family members willing to take part in yet another one of Cari's Odd Ideas.

We made a picnic lunch one summer morning, went to a local park, and with the muddy, silty water of Kensington Lake, Lotus was fake-baptized in a ceremony that made no mention of God. Not God the Father, nor God the Son, nor God the Holy Spirit. This meant that in reality, she wasn't baptized at all, but it made me feel I was doing something very deep and spiritual.

Despite my attempts to conjure up a feel-good relationship with God founded entirely on my whims and self-absorption, He was waiting patiently behind the scenes, offering me genuine opportunities to get to know Him, and calling me, gently and persistently, by my name.

Basement Birds

My whining to the contrary, it wasn't all spiritual crises in our first years as young parents. There were frequent moments of levity, which have to be grabbed and fawned over; otherwise you miss the point of parenthood.

Rugrats

When we bought our house, the basement was unfinished. Nothing but aqua cinderblock and some ceiling tile that was definitely full of asbestos. While I was pregnant with Lotus, we employed as many people as possible to turn that damp, silverfish-infested zone into a family room. Electricity got wired in. Drywall got put up. A bar was built, a computer room created, and paint chosen, and then rechosen when the first-round pick was a disaster.

It was lovely. I have so many happy memories of our little family in that space, watching Lotus go from infant, to sitting up, to crawling around, seemingly in a shorter time than it took for her to gestate.

Late in her first winter, the birds came.

Lotus and I were down in the basement, watching TV and playing together. All of a sudden, one of our greyhounds, who was normally so silent and so lazy you couldn't be entirely sure he was still alive without checking for breathing, jumped up and started barking wildly at something behind me. I whirled around to figure out what was going on just in time to see a smallish black shape fly at my head.

Simultaneously screaming and grabbing Lotus, I was halfway up the stairs before I realized what was going on. Somehow, inexplicably, a starling had gotten into our basement and was frantically flying around.

I didn't care. I ran the rest of the way up the steps, slammed the door at the top, and locked it, leaving my dogs to duke it out with the wayward bird on their own. Lotus looked at me and giggled. She pointed at the door and clapped her hands. Behind it, I could hear the dogs barking, barking at the bird.

Eventually, Ken got home and we spent a very tense fifteen minutes figuring out how to get the stupid bird out of the basement[8] and then congratulated ourselves on a professional-grade pest removal.

Two days later, it happened again! Another basement bird, another terrified exodus, another slamming (and locking!) of the stairway door. Lotus thought the whole thing hilarious. I thought it Hitchcockesque. Finally, we realized the problem —our chimney was missing a mesh screen to cover the hole. When birds would gather around it to soak up the heat coming out, they'd inhale carbon monoxide, pass out, tumble down the chimney, and wake up in our basement.

True story.

Well, a two-dollar wire screen and a short trip up the roof later, our bird problem was fixed. But I couldn't shake the image of birds, trying to stay warm, poisoning themselves. I imagined their confusion and panic when they came to, trapped in a completely foreign environment, unable to escape.

Ken and I were starting to feel like those birds. Both of us were starting to feel as if our jobs, things that we needed for our survival like heat-seeking birds in a Michigan winter, were poisoning us. The source of my agony was having to leave Lotus. Although my parents watched her the first year, and a private babysitter the next, for me the pain of leaving her behind every day never got any easier. The slightest thing would set me crying, sorrowful over the fact that I was paying someone money for the privilege of raising my daughter. I was barely present at work. I started getting severe stomach pains Sunday afternoon,

---

[8] Turn off all lights in the house. Turn on the porch light. Open the back door. Bird will fly toward the light, up the stairs, through the kitchen, and out the door into the night. Good riddance, bird.

thinking about Monday morning. I desperately wanted to be able to stay home and raise her, but there was no way we could afford to go down to one income. So there I sat, hovering over an open chimney for warmth, filling myself with poison.

Ken's troubles with work stemmed from politics and being passed over for a promised promotion—repeatedly. His work environment grew steadily more unbearable until one day in late summer he came home in a fury and angrily said to me, "I wish I could just put in for a transfer."

He was irritably pacing the living-room floor, and I looked up at him from my seat on the couch. "So why don't you?" I asked. He stopped.

"You wouldn't mind?" he asked, hardly daring to hope.

I shrugged and picked up Lotus. "Where would we go?"

"I could see if the warehouse in Memphis is taking any transfers," he said, excitement starting to creep into his voice. "That would be perfect. We'd be close to my parents, the cost of living is so much lower that you could stay home with the kids ..."

The kids. Plural. I had been making occasional comments about being ready for another baby. Lotus was two now, and it seemed like her babyhood was over. But Ken wasn't quite ready. "One is good. I like one," he'd say whenever I brought up the topic. But now, with his use of the word kids, whether intentional or not, I perked up.

"Do it," I said, looking at Lotus and thinking what a great big sister she'd make. I'd move anywhere, if it meant I could stay home with my kids.

Three months later, I was pregnant, homeless, and temporarily living with my parents, since the transfer had gone through much quicker than we had expected. Ken was needed down in Memphis, so I had to tie up loose ends in Michigan.

The house was sold, the news of my resignation broken to my principal, and a new baby was rapidly dividing cells and forming organs in the darkness of my body.

It was as if someone had covered the screen of the chimney we had been hovering over and, instead of letting us sit there, sucking in the poison, shooed us away with a massive, cosmic hand.

When I had finally settled in Memphis, I came to know the owner of that hand, as I had been longing to do my whole life.

Part 2

∞

Mississippi

3

∞

Lost in Translation

Memphis is near the state line between Tennessee and Mississippi. We found that we could afford significantly more house in Mississippi than across the border in Tennessee, so Ken confined his house hunting to the Magnolia State.

He had been living at his parents' house during the months Lotus and I were closing up shop in Michigan, and the day we took possession of the house was two days after I got down to Memphis. He drove me to see the house for the first time, keys in hand, and I about died when I saw the neighborhood. It was, in retrospect, a collection of shoddily built McMansions of varying size, but there was a golf course running through the center of the subdivision. In my mind, this made the whole thing inconceivably fancy. Certainly, if that neighborhood had been in Michigan, it wasn't a place we'd ever be able to afford.

I walked into my new house and started mentally unpacking. The nursery would go in this room; Lotus would have that room over there; the couch would go angled just so. It was all so grand that it took me a full hour to notice the state of the carpet.

It was disgusting. Huge, ominous stains in highly visible areas that no piece of furniture could easily hide. I pointed this out to my husband, and he responded with a huge grin.

"I negotiated a professional carpet cleaning in the contract!" he said proudly. I looked around with a satisfied eye. A professional carpet cleaning on the seller's dime would be just the thing. We nodded and grinned at each other like a pair of loons, loaded Lotus into the car, and headed back to Ken's parents' house.

As Ken sped along the long country roads, I called a local carpet-cleaning company someone had recommended.

"Auuhyah. Wiiiynston's caaaaarpeet surr-usus." I paused and turned toward Ken with my mouth agape.

Unable to parse a glimmer of meaning from that sound, I said, "Pardon?"

"Huh?" came the response.

"I'm trying to call Winston's Carpet Services. Is this the correct number?" Ken glanced at me, then back at the road.

"Huh? Thaaaaaaays is Wiiiiiiynston's, maaaaaa'aaam," I pulled the phone from my ear to check how many bars of service I was getting.

"I'm sorry, Winston's? Um, I need to schedule a carpet cleaning? What's the soonest time you have available?"

From the other end came more unintelligible braying. I repeated myself anxiously. "Carpet cleaning. I need to schedule one." More noise. "Pardon?" I said.

"Huh?" came the other end.

"Pardon?"

"Huh?" Surely this was a joke.

Ken looked at me again. "Slow down. You're speaking like a northerner. They can't understand you."

I stuck my tongue out at him. "I *am* a northerner!"

He shrugged. "Well, they're not going to understand you, and we'll never get our carpet cleaned."

He had a point. I took a deep breath and repeated myself. "I ... need ... my car-pet cleaned ... at your ... earliest ... con-veen-ee-ence." I was speaking so slowly I was sure the man at the other end was going to hang up on me, insulted. He didn't. Instead, he said something that I imagined was, "Well, ma'am, tomorrow at 9:30 a.m. is our earliest appointment. Would that work for you?" but really sounded like, "Maaa'aaamm weeerwoigouiiouwe weoirw rreooooigughese?" and I said, "Sure, we'll be there," and mercifully ended the phone call.

Ken was chuckling.

He drawled slowly, "Huh-nee ... Thay'err gown-ta put yee-ou in the nerr-vous haws-spital ... if yee-ou keep taww-kin' laaahk thay-at." I punched him softly on the arm as we made our way through a Mississippi back road, with dusk falling over dormant farmland and winter-brown creek beds.

In Which I Am Repeatedly Asked a Rude Question and Finally Forced to Answer It, Despite the Chemtrails

Those first few months down south were intense. From the bubbas and their monster trucks congregating at Wal-Mart, to people walking around in 65-degree weather bundled up to the chin in heavy coats and scarves, to the first completely cloud-less skies I had seen in my entire life, I felt as if I had fallen through Alice's Looking Glass.

A shockingly bad combination of culture shock and preg-nancy hormones produced what I can describe only as temporary psychosis. For a solid four months, I became obsessed with the conspiracy theory of *chemtrails*. This is the notion that the gov-ernment or some paragovernment agency was using airplanes to deliberately douse the population with chemicals.[9] I found myself unwilling to go outside very often, or for very long. I would have been very happy to stay holed up in the house with Lotus and the dogs, quietly growing my second child, but for the agonizing rudeness of my new neighbors.

Let me explain. Southern hospitality is a very real thing. Within a week of moving in, we had met every single family on our street. They came with flawless charm and goodwill, bearing some housewarming gift, and the conversation went absolutely the same every time:

"Hi! I'm So-and-so, your neighbor two doors down on the left! It's nice to meet you!"

Here I would accept the baked good or plant, tell my name, and invite them into my house, which was in mid-unpacking shambles. The neighbor would politely decline to come in, to my extreme gratitude (see what I mean about Southern hospitality?), and would continue: "So, have you found a church yet?"

No. I am not kidding you. This was the first question from everyone. As if they could see right into my heart and knew the one question that would cause me the most discomfort. Had I found a church yet? I hadn't even found a *religion* yet!

I grew up in the Midwest, where you do not talk about politics, money, or religion with mere acquaintances. It was partly this reluctance to discuss God that had let me coast this far

---

[9] Chemicals designed to do anything from cause cancer to infertility to immediate death, depending on which website you visit. What mere pilots and weathermen call condensation trails or "contrails" coming from the tail-pipes of jets, leaving a white trail of condensed water behind a jet, we conspiracy initiates know to be deadly chemicals strong enough to enslave or kill the entire U.S. population.

without coming to any conclusions. But in the South, people keep God—specifically Christianity—right there in the open.

The oil-change place down the road had on its scrolling marquee, "$2 off oil change with your church's Sunday bulletin." The numerous nondenominational worship centers with curious names like "CrossPointe" and "Life Fellowship" would send glossy postcards in mass mailings, inviting the whole town to a new sermon series. Church was as much a part of your private and public life as your job. And so, while I viewed it as a horrifically rude question, my neighbors were being nothing but friendly when they asked me about my church affiliation.

One day, in a fit of agitation, I called my mom to whine to her about the mean neighbors who were in my face about church. She very sensibly suggested that next time someone asked me what church I went to, I respond by saying that Ken and I were married in a Presbyterian church and play the odds that the other person would be Baptist or Apostolic Pentecostal, would assume I had found a suitable replacement church already, and would then leave me alone.

Brilliant! It worked like a charm. No longer did I have to worm out of uncomfortable front-porch religious talks by "accidentally" letting my dogs escape. Now I could mention "Presbyterian wedding" and be left in peace.

Until I met the neighbors directly across the cul-de-sac —the last to introduce themselves. Who were, of course, Presbyterian. Who then offered to have the pastor of their church come over one day so we could meet him. Who started calling every few days to see if I had checked with Ken to figure out a good time to do so. I was backed into a corner. Why did they keep trying to jam their *Christian God* down my throat? Couldn't they take a hint?

Finally, the fear of church was so strong in me, I made a difficult decision. Chemtrails be damned, I had to get out of the house. I had to find some way to avoid these neighbors, even if it meant exposing my pregnant self and my two-year-old daughter to the cocktail of carcinogens clearly being dumped on us by sinister global organizations.

So I did. Every day, I made a point to leave the house, generally about fifteen minutes before I expected the neighbors to get home from work. Lotus and I would go to the library, or to Wal-Mart, or to my in-laws' house across the state line in Tennessee. Each time I drove around under those perfectly-blue-except-for-the-chemtrails skies, I felt myself growing more and more fond of my new home. It really was beautiful. Winter was mild, and by late February, practically over. My cousin came to visit, and I dragged her to Graceland, where we stared in horrified fascination at Elvis's shag carpet-covered bed and Lisa Marie's depressingly shabby swing set. The people were quick to smile, slow to get angry, and willing to share what they had. I was, in fact, being lulled into a trap.

The trap was sprung one day in early March. Lotus was down for a nap, and I was giving serious consideration to doing the same when there was a knock at the door. Feeling very sleepy and docile, I went to answer it.

My Presbyterian neighbor! I recoiled a little, shocked into sensibility. I had no escape route!

As my neighbor politely began talking about her church again and telling me how much her pastor was looking forward to meeting my family, I found myself desperately wishing that Lotus would wake up from her nap, preferably howling. I tried to psychically poke her into a screaming fit. She stubbornly remained silent.

Backed into a corner by her graciousness, I heard myself suddenly blurting out, "You know, Ken's parents are Presbyterian, and I think we're going to start checking out their church." Oh, God—had I just said that? Please tell me I'd just said that mentally and not actually out loud.

"They are? That's great!" Nope. Obviously I'd said it out loud. "You guys will get to worship together as a family!" She was genuinely happy about this turn of events. Giving me a smile, she waved and walked back home, never to bring up the subject of her church again.

I stared after her, watching her cross the cul-de-sac, walk up her driveway, and disappear into her house. My insane, rash words were still there, though, filling up the room around me. Now that I had said I was going to go to a church, I had to make good on it at least once, just so I wasn't a liar. (Somehow, lying about God while claiming to search for Him seemed a spectacularly bad idea.)

Now I had to do some serious—something. *Something.* I didn't even know what. All I knew was that I had this giant chip on my shoulder regarding all things Christian, and it was starting to get very heavy. I had given every other religious system a fair shot. I realized that it was finally time to apply my nonnegotiables to Christianity and eliminate it from consideration the way I had done all other organized religions. It seemed fair.

So, starting with the notion of not being willing to worship a created object, I turned the powers of the Internet to the question of Christ. Christ, whom I had firmly shut out of our wedding, was, as I understood Him to be, a creature. After all, He was the Son of the Father, and sons are creatures, so this should be pretty cut and dried.

At the time, Ken was working particularly grueling hours. He left for work around two in the afternoon and didn't get back until four in the morning. Plus, he worked most Saturdays. So to say that this left me, a young, pregnant mother, a stranger in a new town, with a bit of free time is an understatement. I had ample opportunity to research Christianity out of consideration.

One evening, after Lotus had been bathed and put to bed, the house cleaned, the dogs brushed, the garden weeded, and no chores left to distract me, I sat down in front of the computer to check the Internet's understanding of the nature of Christ.

The top search result directed me to the first chapter of the Gospel of St. John, specifically the first few verses. Then it helpfully suggested a website where I could read these verses in about a million translations:

> In the beginning was the Word,
> and the Word was with God,
> and the Word was God.

You know the phrase "my blood ran cold"? You're so scared, it's as if your blood has turned to ice water.

There is an opposite feeling, but I don't know if there's an idiom for it. It's when you're suddenly so overwhelmed with a sense of safety that your blood feels as if it's made of *sunlight*. That's what I felt when I read those words in John.

I didn't understand it. Don't get me wrong. I'm not a Bible scholar, and I'm certainly not a theologian, but I was able to glean one thing: *Christianity doesn't teach that Christ was a created thing.* He was in existence from before time, with God Himself.

Immediately following on the heels of that discovery was one even more meaningful for me. Christ was a Word. A *Word.* He was the conversation God wanted to have with me about Himself, a conversation He had waited so patiently to have—while I flailed about like a three-year-old having a Halloween sugar-crash temper tantrum, kicking the kitchen floor and sticking my fingers in my ears, alternating screams of "Talk to me!" and "I'm not listening!"

I sat there for a while, staring at the computer screen. All this time I had wanted God to speak to me. Then I went around doing things like censoring His Word from my wedding. I should have been ashamed. Instead I was astounded. I was astounded that Christianity doesn't involve worshipping created beings as is done in New Age or Hindu traditions. I was astounded that its holy writings were enthusiastically translated into every written language—with no claims to a loss of clarity because of it—unlike Islam.

With the first of my nonnegotiable hurdles cleared, I was ready to make good on my promise to visit a church. I now looked forward to seeing what else Christianity and its Christ could reveal.

I Step into a Church Again
and Do Not Burst into Flames

When I told Ken that I—and by extension, *he*—was honor bound to attend one service at his parents' church, he was nonchalant. A lifetime of familiarity with my spiritual wandering had rendered him pretty much immune to my religious proclamations, and he called his parents to tell them that we'd be meeting them at church that Sunday.

I got ready to go pay the piper, irritated and on edge. Here I was, full circle, going to a Presbyterian worship service. Time and space may be different, but that was it. All the same questions I had had as a child crowded around me—who was God? What did He want from us? How were we to know the path to Him?

These questions, coupled with a dark, grimly amusing fear that I was going to burst into flame upon entering Germantown Presbyterian Church, made for an unpleasant drive to meet my in-laws. When we got there, we were directed to the nursery, where Lotus could be dropped off. Someone handed Ken a beeper in case there was a problem, and so my best escape route was neatly taken from me.

There was nothing left to do but sit down and shut up.

I'm not sure what I expected to find in that first church service since Ken and I were married. The people were gracious and welcoming; the music was tasteful, and the pastor's sermon was engaging. And best of all, it was followed by brunch at my in-laws' country club. There were no extremes here. I didn't spontaneously combust, but neither did I receive any divine revelations. It was a low-key, nonthreatening experience that Ken and I were willing to recreate on future Sundays.

But my heart still wasn't settled. So at nights, with the baby asleep and Ken at work, I continued my obsessive searching on the Internet. I wanted to know more about Christianity, and I wasn't even sure what I wanted to learn.

During my searches, I fell down rabbit holes constantly. I'd begin researching what the Presbyterian church currently taught about predestination, for example, and somehow find myself on a web page offering to make me an ordained minister in the Universal Life Church Monastery through a simple click of the mouse. Or I'd run an innocent search on the church down the road from me, whose marquee encouraged passersby to "COME AND LEARN THE TRUTH ABOUT ISLAM," only to wind up reading a fascinating post about why the King James translation is the only authentic version of the Bible—better even than the original Hebrew and Greek! The Internet was both a blessing and a curse for an ADD case like me.

But then one day, roughly half an hour down the rabbit hole, I came across a painting, *The Virgin, Jesus, and Saint John Baptist* (1875), by William-Adolphe Bouguereau. In the picture, Mary sits on a marble throne, barefoot, with the Infant on her lap. Next to her, happily leaning against her crossed legs, is a young John the Baptist, no more than five, wearing a camel-skin tunic. John and Jesus are happily embracing, having the best of times. What stopped me dead in my tracks, though, is the look on Mary's face. The set of her lips and placement of her fingers against her cheek bespeaks a fiercely protective mother.

Her gaze, locked with laser-like intensity on Christ, says, "I will never let you out of my sight, for you are all I want to see."

I stared at that picture and realized what I wanted. I wanted to have the same focus on God that Mary has in that painting. I wanted that iron will, unshakably fixed on God. I wanted a faith that was, like Mary's, epic. And once I had articulated this in my heart, I knew somehow that Mary herself would lead me there. I was filled with complete trust that if I followed her example, she would show me how to love God and how to establish that relationship with Him I had been longing for my whole life.

Now, *finally*, I had a focus in my search. I just had to copy Mary long enough to figure out where I was supposed to go. I thought of it as shadowing someone on the job. Only it was like shadowing someone on a job for which I didn't know the location, language, or purpose.

Where does one start following Mary? In my childhood, Mary was dutifully trotted out for Christmas, to bear the Savior in a stable after being told there was no room in the assorted inns. Then she was gone, not to be heard from until next Christmas. Our time in Michigan, a block away from St. Sabina's, taught me that she was readily visible in statue form, but that didn't seem to help.

Miserably and reluctantly, I turned to the Bible. For the first time, I was now reading it with an eye for actual instruction — rather than mining it for the "weird parts" the way I did as a child, to distract myself during particularly boring sermons.

But the more I read, the more I became comfortable with Christ. He stopped being a sticking point with me, someone I viewed as "standing in the way of my relationship with God." He started being Someone who loved me — Someone who demonstrated what God's love meant, in a way that a weak and limited human being could understand. Until I saw God as a human, I never appreciated how impossible it is for man to grasp the immensity of God's commitment to us.

I spent much of my plentiful free time scanning the landscape for more information about this Person who loved me so much that He wanted to spend all eternity with me — wanted it enough to endure torture and death for my salvation. For a woman with a lifelong, dramatic love affair with her husband, this sort of display of emotion was very, very attractive.

I Hit a Few Bumps in the Road

I honestly thought that once I came this far in my spiritual journey, the hard part would be over. There was probably a part of me that felt I deserved a ticker-tape parade and a national holiday — "Hurray! Cari's found God!"

But that's not what happened. Instead of things getting clearer once I realized Christianity was the answer to my general questions, they got murkier. I lived, after all, in the Bible

Belt—a place where someone with a theological vision and a few people willing to share it could start his own church in an empty storefront at a strip mall. There were more than a dozen Christian denominations within a five-mile radius of my house—each claiming to have the corner on the truth. It was enough to make a person insane.

Insanity is the only defense I can plead for what happened next. One night, during another of my Internet goose chases, I landed on a website promoting something called the Miraculous Medal. Because I had been raised sensibly Protestant, the notion of medals was foreign to my mind. This was some sort of Catholic tchotchke that I had been warned against, so I should have just clicked away.

But something made me stay. Something made me stay at the site and read what it had to say about itself. And as soon as I realized that this … *thing*—whatever it was—dealt with Mary, I paused. After all, it was Mary whom I was supposed to be copying until I got my footing on Christian ground. It was Mary and her focus on Christ that I sought to emulate. What, I reasoned, could be the harm in looking at this site?

I didn't understand half of what I read. "Extraordinary graces," "sacrament," "Immaculate Conception." Each of these phrases had the air of mystery about it, and it was with a bemused spirit that I clicked on the button that said, "Get a free medal." I mean, I "knew" that Catholics worshipped Mary and all, and that their early missionaries had assimilated so many concepts and symbols from European pagans that they were practically New Agers,[10] but I couldn't figure out this medal thing.

---

[10] Which I wrote about at length in a midterm paper for one of my anthropology classes in college: "Pagan Symbolism in

The Association of the Miraculous Medal, the folks who maintained this puzzling site, claimed that those who wore the thing "devoutly" would receive "great graces." Yet they insisted that it wasn't a magic charm or superstition. I wasn't convinced. However, the prayer circling the medal's image, "O Mary, Conceived without Sin, Pray for Us Who Have Recourse to Thee," resonated with me deeply. I wanted to get to Christ, but I had this ocean of baggage between us. I viewed Mary as a sort of lifeboat that would safely carry me through the unknown waters, bringing me to her Son. Clearly, I had recourse to her, and I would take all the prayers she was willing to offer.

Almost immediately after ordering a medal for myself, I blocked the entire embarrassing incident from my mind and clicked away to something else. No one would have to know that, for a moment, I had fallen in with magic-medal-wearing Catholics.

We kept going to Ken's parents' church, but on a cautious, every-other-week schedule. I needed to keep things at arm's length until I found a place that no longer felt like a compromise. And everything about Protestantism felt like a compromise.

Maybe it was just a matter of finding the denomination that offered the least troubling compromise. But which denomination would that be? There were no fewer than thirteen churches within a five-mile radius of my house—four Baptist, two Apostolic Pentecostal, one Methodist, and the other six nondenominational.

Here was where I started beating my head against my desk at night. This church over here proclaimed on its website that

---

Roman Catholicism and Other Branches of Christianity." I considered myself an expert in the field.

infant baptism was a heresy, while this other church's website was diplomatically neutral on the subject. One church insisted that baptism by full immersion was the only way you could join them, while another site ignored all mention of baptism. And that was just the concrete stuff. Once you got to theories of justification and sanctification and the nature of sin, things either spun off into a million directions, or else you had a mushy-sounding mission statement about "all are welcome and we're not here to focus on sin, but rather growing relationships with God through very elaborate Sunday music concerts. And sermon series."

I grew steadily horrified by the implications of what I was learning. If something as necessary and fundamental as baptism couldn't be agreed on—something so basic that even a wandering pagan would strive to imitate it with her infant child—how were we mortals supposed to know when we were getting any of it right?

But with that image of Mary and her unblinking focus on Jesus in mind, I kept on. I had read in the Bible that Jesus promised that the gates of Hell wouldn't prevail against His Church, so I figured that somewhere, I'd find where that church was.

As I puzzled through that, I was also trying to get a clear answer about why I should go to church at all. When Christ said He was establishing a church, did He really mean an actual, physical structure? Couldn't I spend Sunday out in nature, giving thanks for God's creation, and be engaging in worship? After all, what did I find at church that was found exclusively there?

In my more childish moments, I got angry. Why would God do this? Why would He plant this longing in my heart to come to Him, to know Him, and then not reveal a clear path?

Was He some sort of sadist? Did He just like tricking people? It seemed ridiculous to me that there wasn't an unbroken trail that we could follow throughout history to get our miserable selves to God.

Are Roman Catholics Christians?

A few weeks later, I was at one of the Tuesday story times at the library, taking Lotus to the bathroom. On the counter, next to the sink, was a stack of rectangular booklets. While I waited for Lotus, I idly picked one up. The cover, red and black, with a picture of a rosary on one side, was both visually striking and troubling. There was something in the cover—maybe the color choice—that suggested Nazism. The title was even more perplexing: "Are Roman Catholics Christians?" I paused at this, because the pamphleteers let me know that they didn't think so. There was something so grotesque in the presentation that I couldn't tear my eyes away.

Lotus came out of the bathroom stall, and I hastily shoved the pamphlet in my pocket, instinctively shielding her from seeing the stack of them by the sink as I helped her wash her hands and hurriedly ushered her from the bathroom back to story time, my thoughts a million miles away.

That night, after Lotus was tucked away in bed, I retrieved the booklet from where I'd stashed it behind a stack of bills, feeling a strange, primal sense of revulsion for the thing. I flipped through it, feeling dirtier and dirtier the more I read. There was a repulsive evil coming off the pages of this pamphlet.

Now, let me explain some things. Despite the fact that I had grown up with Catholic friends, had a Catholic godfather, and had attended Catholic funeral and wedding Masses, I had never, even for a fleeting second, considered Catholicism as a possible contender for the religious truth God was trying to show me.

I grew up in a household that was firmly pro-"choice" and decidedly anti–any establishment other than a labor union. In my mind, the Catholic Church was about hate—hatred of women, hatred of sex, hatred of non-Catholics, hatred of science. In fact, although Mary was my guide on my search through Christianity, Catholicism never once appeared on my radar. How could it? How could I consider a patriarchal religion that was so firmly out of touch with the modern world?

And yet, reading through that ugly little tract, which vomited a level of hatred for the Church that far exceeded my own stupid complaints, I was indignant. I was offended on behalf of a Church I knew nothing about. For no other reason than to disprove the wild accusations of a poorly executed religious comic, I found myself turning my Internet searches to Catholicism. Not to explore the possibility that it held answers to my questions, but simply to stick it to Chick Publications, the company that proudly published the booklet.

I stashed the dirty little comic away deep in the recesses of my desk, praying that no one else would stumble across it, and went to bed, thinking on how to best begin my debunking project.

Ostrich Boots

Days passed. During the day I'd fill my time with house-cleaning chores and day trips with Lotus. Sometimes I'd go to the OB I had reluctantly picked, and those days always ended with me in tears.

The doctor did not have a good bedside manner. He was very brusque and negative, and would constantly remind me that his C-section rate was 10 percent lower than Brazil's, which neared the 90-percent mark. No matter how many times I reminded him that this wasn't, in fact, Brazil, he didn't listen. In fact, "didn't listen" summed up his whole professional persona. When I was in there, I was filled with the sense that I was little more than an object in his mind—a pregnant object that was to be endured for the sake of a paycheck.

Finally, after the third appointment in a row where I returned home in that volatile mix of rage and hysterics, Ken suggested I find a new doctor. I countered with demands for a midwife, since I didn't want any C-section butcher to lay hands on me ever again. Too smart to get into a debate with a hormonal wife in her second trimester, Ken told me to start looking for a midwife.

I found one the next day, and over the phone she told me that she'd send her information packet in the mail. In the meantime, she suggested that I make an appointment with the OB whom she worked with, just to get things started.

I did just that, and there I met my second-favorite OB of all time. The doctor was tall, thin, wore ostrich-skin cowboy boots, and used the phrase, "Whoa Nellie!" a lot. I loved him. He was low-key, personable, and sat down at the end of the appointment to ask me if I had any questions. Never once did he mention Brazil.

4

∞

Jack Chick Leads Me to the Eucharist

The issue of an OB finally settled, I was able to stop searching for acceptable prenatal care and return to my late-night Internet research on the sordid accusations in the Chick tract. During my college years, my spiritual quest had taken me deep into pagan and occult territory, through the pantheons of Egyptian, Greek, and European deities, past Wicca and witchcraft, and alongside metaphysical-Hindu hybrids. I had spent hours and hours in the library at Michigan State, reading books about papal scandals, books about Catholicism's pagan roots, and books about the systematic suppression of pagan practices by evil, patriarchal Catholic missionaries. The sort of New Age feminist paganism I was drawn to loved nothing better than railing against the evils of Catholicism, so to read in the Chick tract the assertion that Catholic Communion was nothing but a continuation of Egyptian religious practices seemed suspect.

Looking over the booklet again, I noticed that all the books it cited were written by people attached to Chick publications. Now, when I was deep into New Age practices, the notion of scholarly integrity didn't matter much to me, but as I progressed on my spiritual journey, my critical-thinking skills were undergoing a happy strengthening.

I thought I'd let the Catholics explain themselves. I'd read over what they taught about their Communion and crosscheck it with what Chick said about it.

Only I never got that far.

At that point, all I knew about Catholic Communion was that only Catholics were allowed to receive it. I figured it had to do with controlling believers and keeping them separate from non-Catholics. Once during college, I attended an Ash Wednesday service at the campus parish and received Communion. I'm not sure if I did it maliciously—to stick it to those backward Catholics—or merely out of arrogance. I knew better than they did whom God wanted up there, so I received. No, if I'm going to be honest, I didn't "receive." I took.

With this the total of my knowledge of Catholic Communion, I started reading.

What I found changed everything for me. Forever.

Catholicism taught that Communion wasn't merely a way to remember Jesus and give thanks for His work in a vague sort of memorial. Catholics taught that their Communion—referred to as "the Eucharist"—was *actually Jesus*. Like, for-really-real Jesus. In the flesh. And the blood. And the soul. And the divinity. Catholics believed that at every Mass, every time, everywhere, Jesus came to the faithful as a fragile little wafer and a chalice of poor-quality wine.

At first, I couldn't even wrap my head around this. If this were true, if this were really, honest-to-God true, it would be a miracle. A daily miracle, repeated over and over again, all across the world. It would mean that I could follow Mary right to Jesus, and see Him with my own eyes and hold Him with my own hands and take Him into my body as Mary got to do for nine months.

Jack Chick Leads Me to the Eucharist

It was too much. I backed away from the thought for a little while, since the possibility hurt with its brightness. It was like sitting in a dark movie theater to watch a film, then walking out into the blazing sun of a summer afternoon. Instead, I started skirting around the Eucharist—which I learned was Greek for "thanksgiving"—and taking furtive glances at other aspects of Catholicism from the corners of my eyes. I couldn't look at Communion face on, so I sort of let it hover at the edges of my peripheral vision.

I read a bit about the early Christians, but then I discovered that even from the start of Christianity, there was the same understanding that Communion—the Eucharist—was actually Jesus, so I had to look away. Then I read the astounding statement that Catholicism taught that it contained the fullness of the truth—that while all religions contained some degree of truth, the sum total of what God revealed to humanity was contained within the Catholic Church. To a mind steeped in moral relativism like mine was, this thought was almost as painful as that of the Eucharist, so I flinched again.

I read about how the books in the Bible had been decided on by a Catholic council that understood itself to be under the guidance of the Holy Spirit. I read how for twelve hundred years, Christians read those books with the belief that they were the inspired word of God. Then, as part of his rebellion against the Church, Martin Luther removed some of them, declaring them not inspired.

The more I read, the more I realized that I had been foolish in failing to consider Catholicism. And the more I realized this, the angrier I got. I didn't want Catholicism on the radar. It was a religion of superstition and misogyny and patriarchy. It was stupid, and I wanted it to go away.

So I stopped research for a while. But fluttering constantly at the edges of my thoughts was the question: *What if Jesus really is the Eucharist?*

The Whole Universe
Starts Screaming, "CATHOLIC!"

I put away my thinking cap, but God wouldn't let me off the hook that easily. He had been waiting so patiently for me all these years, calling for me as I fumbled my way through obstacles and barriers of my own making, and now that I was getting close, He wouldn't let me slip away onto another side path.

Suddenly, the whole world seemed to speak about nothing but Catholic issues. Somewhere, three states away, in Florida, a woman named Terri Schiavo was dying. Daily there was chatter on the radio about it. My safe secular world talked about dying with dignity and last wishes and the authority of next of kin, which was all well and good as far as I was concerned. But then there were all these Catholic bishops who just wouldn't shut up about the sanctity of human life, how that life was measured from conception to natural death, and how Terri Schiavo's husband was advocating murder.

I wanted Terri Schiavo to go away, because she had brought the bishops with her. And every time I heard a bishop speaking, I started thinking about Catholic notions of apostolic succession and their claims to an unbroken line all the way back to Peter and the Apostles, and all their continuity and unity and fullness of the truth and the Eucharist. It always came back to the Eucharist.

Then, tragically, Terri Schiavo did go away, murdered by the people she should have been able to count on, and I selfishly thought we'd be able to go back to business as bishop-free usual.

But I was wrong. I was so, so wrong, because then, the world turned its eyes to the final days of Pope John Paul II.

I thought the Catholic problem was bad with the Schiavo case, but it reached intolerable levels during Pope John Paul's deathwatch.

Every day, the Catholic church across the street from my subdivision had its parking lot full to overflowing. As I irritably maneuvered my way past the cars parked on the side of the road, I threw baleful looks at the turquoise-roofed building: "Queen of Peace Catholic Church." With its gaudy tin roof and its ridiculously Catholic name and all those people inside, every day united in grief and prayer over the last days of some old man in Rome, that building became the focal point for my exasperation.

Saturday, April 2, 2005, dawned lovely and clear, the skies absent of both clouds and government-sponsored chemtrails. Ken, Lotus, and I went to run errands, getting odds and ends ready for the new baby, who was set to arrive sometime in the next two months. We stopped for lunch at a local pizza chain that featured TVs on the ceilings, an all-you-can-eat pizza buffet, and an atmosphere so loud that our high-spirited two-year-old wouldn't have to be shushed to spare the digestion of other patrons.

We settled in, and as Ken took Lotus up to the buffet, my eyes drifted to one of the flickering TV screens, and I saw the news.

The sound was muted, so the only way I could make sense of the images was by reading the news ticker crawling across the bottom of the screen. Pope John Paul II, after a very public struggle with Parkinson's, had just died. I read the words, then suddenly started crying.

Right there in the middle of a stupid pizza joint, crying. For a man I didn't know, who was the leader of a Church I didn't want to think about. Crying.

I rushed to the bathroom before Ken and Lotus could come back to the table and ask what I was doing. In the stall in the miraculously empty bathroom, I heaved these startling, deep sobs. I felt as if my heart were breaking over the loss.

I couldn't understand what was going on. I thought it was either pregnancy hormones or some sort of nervous breakdown. While I certainly didn't consider myself to be part of the Chick-Tract Anti-Catholicism Club, I had no love for the Church. One of my favorite phrases, when the subject turned to anything Catholic was "The Church is going to crumble under its own bloated weight. If we're lucky, it'll happen in our lifetime."

This was the woman who found herself sobbing in a bathroom stall over the death of a pope. But, rather than dwell on my possible mental collapse, I pulled myself together, washed my face, and went back to my table, making sure to take a seat with my back to the TV screen.

Conversion Means to Turn

I got really good at ignoring Queen of Peace Catholic Church. This was a stunning testament to the powers of denial when you considered just how huge and how turquoise its tin roof was. I ignored all discussion of the ensuing Papal Conclave. Some odd mention of black smoke and white smoke did creep into my consciousness. But I displayed truly heroic denial.

Then, during an appointment with the ostrich-skin-wearing OB, I was hit with some very bad news.

"Whoa Nellie!" the doctor muttered to himself as he measured me. This pronouncement raised my curiosity only mildly, since he had been saying, "Whoa Nellie!" for the past several appointments. He was prepping me for the possibility that "this one's gonna be a big 'un." But then he turned away from me and started flipping switches on the ultrasound machine at my side.

A short scan later, and he wiped the gel off my shockingly large abdomen, sat down on a stool, and sighed.

"Well, the baby's breech," he said, pointing to the ultrasound picture he had just printed. "And the baby's big. And the due date's close enough that if the baby was going to turn, it would have done so already."

I could hear the blood rushing in my ears. The room got super hot. I didn't know where this conversation was headed, but I wished Doc Ostrich Boots would just get to the point.

Fifteen minutes later, I stumbled to my car and called Ken. With a shaking, teary voice, I told him what the doctor had told me: The baby was breech, and we had two options. One, we could try a version—getting the baby to turn the right way. This sounded scary and painful, and presented a slight possibility that the procedure could hurt the baby or me, and result in an emergency C-section. Or we could go for option two: Skip the version and go straight to a scheduled C-section.

Ken wisely told me just to get home and we'd discuss our options when I wasn't emotional and driving. I agreed, hung up the phone, and promptly called my mom. I had an identical conversation with her, down to the suggestion that I hang up the phone and call her back from home—when I wasn't emotional and driving.

I muttered about so many sensible people on my caller list and drove the rest of the way home, worrying.

Ultimately, Ken and I opted not to try the version. Everything we read gave it a success rate in the 50-percent range, with an emergency C-section waiting at the end of every failed one. Better to schedule the surgery, the better to prep for it.

My mom made plans to fly in at the end of May, which was when it was scheduled, and I spent the last few weeks of the pregnancy feeling very sorry for myself.

One day, with two weeks to go before the C-section, I went out to get the mail. I idly shooed away a sweat bee with the electric bill and puzzled over the mysterious envelope in the mail pile. Professionally printed, but still sort of shabby-looking—sort of like junk mail telling me I was eligible for an exciting new FHA loan—I almost stuck it in the discard pile.

Then I saw the return address: Association of the Miraculous Medal, Perryville, Missouri.

I stopped in my tracks. The sweat bee came back and darted back and forth around my arm. The medal! The ridiculous Catholic medal that I had sent away for—and stupidly provided my real name and address. Unsure what horrors lurked within, I opened the envelope, only to find *another* envelope inside, this one with the phrase "BLESSED OBJECTS INSIDE" in giant blue letters. I opened this second envelope, tipped its contents into my hand, and stared for a moment at the little metal oval, with Mary's image in relief. The words "O Mary, Conceived without Sin, Pray for Us Who Have Recourse to Thee" encircled her.

I stared, transfixed by the thing, trying to puzzle out the cryptic meaning of the prayer. What did it mean? What did any of it mean?

The sound of my neighbor pulling into her driveway snapped me back to myself. Shoving the medal into my pocket, and jumping a little as if I had been caught doing something against the rules, I gave a half-wave to my neighbor and hightailed it into the house, where no one else could see me holding Catholic trinkets in my front yard.

I shoved the envelope way down in the garbage and took the medal out of my pocket, putting it up on a high shelf where it wouldn't accidentally be discovered. Later that night, after I had put Lotus to bed and could tell by the silence coming from her room that she had fallen asleep, I brought the medal down for further inspection.

It was just so ... so *Catholic*. Apart from a neon "CATHO-LIC" sign, I couldn't think of anything more obviously Catholic. But right there, front and center, was Mary. The same Mary whose faith and trust I so admired and sought to copy.

"Okay, Mary," I thought to myself, "I'll put this on, but only because I want to remind myself to stay as close to Jesus as you did. I'll put this on as a sign of my trust that you'll lead me to the place where I'm going to be closest to Him, okay?" I felt as if I needed to make it very clear that this was a sort of guide tool, and not an indication of religious affiliation. I couldn't help it if the Catholics hogged Mary. I needed to follow her to get to her Son, and if the path took me into weird territory, then fine. I had been in weirder places.

I found a chain, slipped the medal onto it, and snapped the hook closed. A Miraculous Medal, there on the neck of a woman raised Presbyterian, who had spent more than a decade entrenched in New Age spirituality, now walking toward Jesus with hesitant, teetering steps, clutching His mom's hand for support.

I tried my best to pretend the medal wasn't there. When Ken saw it, he asked what it was but didn't seem too concerned. When it comes time to open that man's case for sainthood, the calm manner with which he approached my spastic religious rambling will be exhibit A. He never criticized or ridiculed. He just let me poke along at my own pace, and when I had something to share, he'd give it his full attention, offering his opinion only when I asked him for it.

I wasn't asking for his opinion this time.

The day of the C-section grew closer. I imagined all sorts of horrible scenarios, mostly involving me dying. Every time I caught myself slipping down dark daydreams, I'd remember the prayer on the medal: "Pray for Us Who Have Recourse to Thee." I wasn't entirely sure what it meant, and it certainly never dawned on me to ask Mary to pray for the safety of my child and me during the surgery, but the phrase would echo in my head over and over.

My mom had flown in. The day of the operation, I was in a hospital room with her, my mother- and father-in-law, and Ken. They watched me get prepped, keeping smiles on their faces in direct opposition to my increasingly panicked expressions. It was *go* time. Doc Ostrich Boots came in for a final feel of the baby, to double-check where he would make the incision. I kept breathing deeply, trying not to faint from fear.

An odd look came over the doctor's face. He fiddled with my abdomen some more. He muttered under his breath and glanced at me.

"I'll be right back. Don't go anywhere," he said and disappeared into the hallway. I looked at Ken, trying to blink away the tunnel vision that was creeping in. Doc Ostrich Boots came back in, wheeling a machine in front of him. He started it up, squirted that freezing goop on my skin, and pulled out an ultrasound paddle. I looked at him quizzically.

Finally, he turned off the machine, wiped the gel off my stomach, and sat down next to me.

"Why didn't you tell me the baby had turned?" he asked.

I stared at him.

"What?" was the best I could manage.

"The baby. It's turned. When did it happen?" He looked at me intently, as if I were deliberately withholding vital information.

I blinked. I looked around at my family. They were obviously as dumbstruck as I was.

"I don't understand. What?"

Doc Ostrich Boots allowed himself the tiniest of sighs. "The baby. It's turned. It's no longer breech. When did it happen? The baby is very large, and its turning would have been extremely painful for you. When did it happen?"

I shook my head. "I don't know. I didn't feel anything. The … the baby's turned?"

Now it was his turn to look blindsided. "You honestly didn't feel anything?"

I shook my head again. Slowly, something dawned on me.

"So. So … if the baby's turned, then we don't have to do the C-section, right?" I felt a tiny, wild hope in my chest.

Doc Ostrich Boots frowned. "No, we don't have to, but don't you want to have the baby today?"

I was already halfway out of bed. "Heck no! I'm out of here!"

Within an hour, we were all eating breakfast at the local Bob Evans, celebrating the C-section that wasn't. I was so busy eating waffles and hash browns and being relieved that I wasn't having my abdomen sliced open, I wasn't thinking about anything else.

It wasn't until much later that I attributed that unexpected, painless turning to our Lady's intercession through the Miraculous Medal.

Polar Bear Paws Do Not Good Midwives Make

Of course, since I turned down the chance to have the baby by C-section, you know I was then doomed to be overdue, right? The due date came and went. A week after, Doc Ostrich Boots hauled me back into the hospital, this time for an induction. We scheduled an induction; they told me to come in the night before to "prep" me.

Next up on the docket of weird was Doc Ostrich Boots doing battle with the nurses over whether I should be allowed food. The good doctor sensibly pointed out that it was only five or six in the evening—it's entirely possible that I could be without food for twenty-four hours if the nurses had their way.

The nurses told him that with an induction, there's always the chance of an emergency C-section, and I would have to have an empty stomach, should that happen.

The doctor led the nurses into the hallway, shut the door, and while I closed my eyes and tried to find my happy place, I could hear the muffled sounds of an argument. An audible "Whoa Nellie!" followed by an open door, and my awesome ostrich-skin-cowboy-booted OB told Ken that the nurses wouldn't give me food, but they couldn't stop him from providing me with some from an outside source. Like Ken.

I loved that doctor.

Ken went home, made me a PB&J, and brought it back to me. Then the nurses at the hospital give me half a dose of Ambien and told me to press the button if I needed anything. "Tra-la, tra-la," they seemed to say as they gave me half a pill and skipped out of the room.

Some undetermined amount of time later, I experienced the first and only genuine hallucinations of my life, courtesy of Ambien. I remember getting up to pee, walking into the bathroom, and finding that *the corners of the room were filled with stacks of champagne-colored, oval balloons.*

I left the bathroom, climbed into my bed, and noticed that several disembodied polar bear paws were helping to tuck me in.

Polar bear paws.

Tucking me in.

I didn't even wonder at that one.

What I *do* wonder is that they prescribe higher doses of this stuff to people. Holy cow. Just holy cow.

The night of weird passed, and the nurses came to check on me in the morning to see how effaced my cervix was.

It wasn't.

They started me on Pitocin—to induce contractions—and left. They'd come back periodically to check my progress (none) and make sure someone wasn't sneaking me food.

The day passed so slowly. There were contractions, but nothing major. Since I was on a Pitocin drip, I couldn't walk around to help move things along. I was strapped to my bed while the nurses continued to up the dosage.

I said to Ken at one point, "This Pitocin stuff is no big deal. The women who complain about it must be major wimps."

Then, twelve hours after the Pitocin was started, Doc Ostrich Boots had had enough. He broke my waters to speed things along.

And then, because this is how things work for me, I felt my first real Pitocin contraction. It was like going from delicate wings of butterflies on my abdomen to a hundred iron fists of death squeezing in unison—all within the space of a heartbeat. It was decidedly uncomfortable. Up until this point, Ken, Lotus, and my mother- and father-in-law were sitting around the room, chatting, playing cards, hanging out.

I asked my father-in-law to take Lotus out of the room for a while, since I couldn't concentrate on labor with a verbally advanced three-year-old prattling next to me nonstop. He took her out, and the nurses dialed up the Pitocin drip to "Dosage: Elephant."

Now it was *really* uncomfortable. And no painkillers.

Lotus and my father-in-law returned. He had taken her to the gift shop and bought her a stuffed orca. Lotus loves all things whale. She was very excited, and kept trying to get me to admire her new toy properly.

She squeezed it, and it began to make sounds.

What it *said* was, "I'm Odella Orca." Just six syllables. But they were uttered in a pitch somewhere between nails on a chalkboard and a posse of screeching harpies.

I asked my in-laws to take Lotus and the Screaming Toy of Death back to their house. I promised we'd call when the baby came.

At this point, partly because I had been on a Pitocin drip for over twelve hours and partly because I was still furious at not being able to eat, I started having the nurses check me after every contraction.

I was getting nowhere.

Seven centimeters.

Seven centimeters.

Seven centimeters.

What had been up to that point a battalion of nurses finally left me alone. They tagged the low man on the totem pole—a quiet, thin Filipino nurse—to stand guard. She was so sweet and kind that, even in the midst of my pain, I couldn't bear to be mean to her. She probably would have given me a PB&J if I had asked her.

Contraction.
Check me.
Seven centimeters.
Contraction
Check me.
Seven centimeters.

I asked for a shot of Stadol, making sure I was actually asking for it out loud and not telepathically, as I had with Lotus. Ken rubbed my feet, and I thought about the Muppets for no particular reason.

Contraction
Check me.
Seven centimeters.
Over and over.

The first shot of Stadol wore off, and like a junkie, I over-enunciated my request for another one. Had to make sure I didn't sound stoned; otherwise they'd cut me off.

My Filipina guardian angel didn't want to give me more, but finally, after I wouldn't concede the point, supplied another fix.

Contraction
Check me.
Seven centimeters.

Then, not two contractions after my second shot of Stadol, there was an obvious change. My head still swimming from the drugs, I said, "The baby's coming. I have to push. Check me."

Surely wishing that she had taken up some other career path, the best nurse at the entire hospital checked me again.

"Oh!" she said, then turned to press the button. Over the intercom, her gentle sweetness managed to bark out, "She's ten centimeters; it's time to push!"

Duh.

I *was* pushing.

Ken and the nurse could try to stop me all they wanted, trying to get me to wait until there were more hands to help, but to heck with it. Down the hallway, I could actually hear the sounds of the nurse brigade running for my room.

The nurses busted in. As they started prepping whatever it is they couldn't have prepped in the seven million hours before, one nurse checked me, told me the baby's head was right there, and the smallest of pushes would be the end.

I pushed.

Out came the baby. *Right on the bed because there was no one there to catch it.*

Someone picked up the tiny body. Through the haze of Pitocin, Stadol, and hunger, I was aware of the baby being held up for me to see. I heard Ken's voice, amused and chuckling,

"Your son is peeing on you, Cari."

A son!

Peeing on me?

The nurses did whatever nurses do with a newborn, my OB finally came in, checked me, checked the baby, said, "Whoa Nellie!" and left.

I got to hold my beautiful new baby while Ken called his parents to deliver the good news.

We had kept the names to ourselves, so everyone he called was learning not only the sex, but also the name for the first time. Every phone call went like this:

Ken: The baby's here. He's a boy. His name is Joaquin. (*Pause.*) Joaquin. (*Pause.*) J-O-A— Yes, J ... J-O-A-Q-U ... What? (*Pause.*) Yes, Q ... J-O-A-Q-U-I-N. Joaquin. Yup, that's how you say that name, "Hwah-KEEN."

Jack Chick Leads Me to the Eucharist

Every phone call went like that. It was hilarious. By the time Ken called his granny in Texas, he had the whole comedy of errors memorized. But with her, the call went more like this:

Ken: Hi, Granny. The baby's here. He's a boy. His name is Joaquin. You spell it— (*Pause.*) Yeah, you got it! That *is* how you spell it!

Granny, being a die-hard Texas Rangers fan, didn't need anyone spelling *Joaquin* for her. Joaquin Benoit was the Rangers' pitcher, and Granny never missed a game.

My in-laws and Lotus arrived, got to meet the newest addition to the Clan, and didn't even get peed on.

Lucky.

5

∞

Running Home

I'm not actually an Internet troll, hunched over my computer and grumbling angrily.

When I was in middle school, I joined the track team. My mom took me to get all the gear—shoes, sweat suit,[11] obligatory physical, the whole nine yards. She dropped me off at practice the first day, and when she came to pick me up a couple of hours later, I told her I didn't want to do track anymore because there was much more running involved than I had anticipated.

I went on to play soccer in high school, and when forced to run, I would do so very reluctantly and with loud protestations. I figured that I was best suited to running only when chased.

Then, sometime after having Lotus, but before moving to Mississippi, I started running again. And I found that I liked it. I was awful at it, but it didn't matter, since I had fun. Ken and I participated in two triathlons, I ran a couple of 5Ks, and by the time I left Michigan, I had developed a moderately serious running habit.

I kept that habit while pregnant with Joaquin, running through the streets of my neighborhood until I was about seven

[11] It was the '80s. Sweat suits were cool.

months along. That's when the feeling that I was going to have a lead watermelon burst out of me if I shuffled one more step won out over the urge to run. My elderly neighbor was relieved, I'm sure. He had taken to coming out on his porch every morning during my pregnant run, shaking his head at me and shouting, "Slow down!"

The upside to mad pregnancy running (besides annoying the neighbors) was that I recovered from Joaquin's birth much faster than I had from Lotus's. Within five weeks, I was back at it, training for a marathon Ken and I had signed up for at Disney World.

All this matters because the combination of late-night Internet research and mid-morning five-milers gave me things to think about and time to do the thinking. Every runner is a philosopher, at least while on the run. I'd think about what I had read about the early history of Christianity, about the compilation of the Bible, how since the beginning of the Church, the understanding that Christ was physically present in the Eucharist was the norm, and it wasn't until the Protestant Reformation that denying that fact gained any real foothold.

Over and over again, everything came back to the Eucharist. What if the Catholics were right? What if that really *is* Jesus there, the King of the Universe, come to us as bread? I tried to wrap my mind around that, but it seemed like a fever dream. It would present itself as the most obvious of facts; then it would shift, and I found myself recoiling at the implications.

I'd run and run, having debates with myself as I logged the miles. When I needed a break from thinking about the Eucharist, I'd craft objections to the Papacy, the all-male priesthood, and what I understood to be the Church's loathing of human sexuality.

At night, I'd do more research, trying to find holes and flaws in the case for Catholicism that was slowly building all around me. If you'd asked me then if I were running to or away from the Church, I honestly wouldn't have been able to tell you. I was running, that's all I knew.

I Open My Mouth, and the Holy Spirit Comes Out

After hearing ads for it nonstop on Memphis radio, I had finally been to the website, GodSaidManSaid.com, half a dozen times. Each time, I threw up my hands in exasperation. As far as I could tell, the point of the website was to convince people that the only trustworthy, inspired version of the Bible is the King James Version.

If that were true, it would mean two things:

1) Every single person who has been guided by Scripture prior to the publication of the KJV has been led by someone other than God, which means ...

2) That whole thing Jesus promised St. Peter about the gates of Hell not prevailing against His Church? A hollow boast. A lie. After all, if fifteen hundred years' worth of Christians had been misled, wouldn't that mean Hell had, in fact, prevailed?

This was where the whole thing always broke down for me. It wasn't really about that particular website. It was the endless variations of Protestant theology, dogma, and fashions that were driving me insane. If Jesus told us that His Church wouldn't be defeated by Hell and had then spent a great deal of time praying for unity for His Church, how did we end up *here*? If only there were some sort of central authority—some divinely protected clearing house of information to help the faithful navigate their way through the waters of daily life.

And that's when the Papacy started to make sense. Even if I didn't agree with it yet, the necessity for it became crystal clear. We had a Savior who didn't live capriciously. Every moment of His life on earth was rife with meaning and purpose. Why would He leave His Church subject to the whims and fancies of time and culture?

Really, it was all over for me at this point, although I didn't fully see it. I spent time learning all I could about the Papacy —both what Catholics taught about it and the accusations leveled against it by outsiders. My trifecta of spirituality at the time was in full force—research, running, and badgering Mary for insight. If Christ had in fact set up a central authority in His Church, then all the objections I had to things like an unmarried, all-male clergy or bans on birth control were problems with my understanding, not Christianity.

It was a horrifying and humbling prospect.

One day, as we were driving back from Ken's parents' house, Joaquin started crying in the backseat. I crawled into the seat next to him and comforted him. My three-year-old daughter was next to me, staring out the window, and I followed her line of sight—Queen of Peace Catholic Church, with its giant, turquoise, tin roof, dominated the view out the right side of the car. Ken slowed down, put on his turn signal, and waited to pull into our neighborhood.

Everything seemed to slow down and become crystallized with perfect, radiant clarity. In the rearview window, Ken's eyes met mine.

"I think I want to become Catholic," I said, apropos of absolutely nothing.

His sea-blue eyes didn't even blink. "Okay," he said, as if I had just announced that I wanted Mexican for dinner. We drove the rest of the way home in contented silence.

RCIA = *Real Catholic Ignorance Abounds*

Ken agreed to come meet with a priest with me, so I started awkwardly placing calls, completely clueless as to what the protocol was for conversion to the Catholic Church.

I started with Queen of Peace. I called the office one day and spoke with the secretary.

"I. Um. My husband and I want to ... you know. Convert? And I was wondering how we go about doing it?" A long silence at the other end.

"Have you two been baptized?" was the response. Oh! I knew this one!

"Yup. We're both baptized. We were, um, married in a Presbyterian church?" I thought maybe this would help clear up any confusion.

"Well, RCIA classes start in two weeks. They meet every Thursday night from 7:30 to 8:30 in the parish social hall."

My heart sank. Thursday night. 7:30 to 8:30? Ken worked from two in the afternoon until about four in the morning, Monday through Saturday. There was no way he could get off an hour or so every Thursday. And the thought of going through this process without my husband was a nonstarter.

"Oh. Um ... Are there any other churches around? That maybe have their ... um ... classes at a different time?" I could almost feel the secretary shrug at the other end.

"You can try Christ the King in Southaven," she said in a bored voice. I thanked her and hung up. Okay. Christ the King, up next.

I got the same response from Christ the King. RCIA classes were only held on weekday nights. I let out a sad sigh.

"Would you like me to add you to the list?" the man on the other end asked. I thanked him, but told him no, I needed a class that met in the mornings or on weekends.

"Where do you live?" the man asked. I told him, and he suggested I try Queen of Peace.

"I already did," I said, feeling as if I was going to cry. "Their class only meets on Thursday nights, and they told me to try you." There was an irritated sigh on the other end, which I thought was directed at me.

"Priests have to work with …" his voice trailed off angrily. "Let me call Queen of Peace. I'll talk to the priest over there. If you can't make RCIA classes, someone will meet with you privately." Finally realizing that the irritation wasn't directed at me, and that this man, whoever he was, was going to help, I thanked him ten million times and hung up the phone.

Within a day, the priest at Queen of Peace called me and arranged for private meetings that Ken and I could attend together. I couldn't wait. There was so much I was ignorant about, I didn't even know what to expect. How did this work? Did we have to pass a test before we could be let into the Church? What was on the test? Would we get a study guide? What if we failed? Was there a retest?

For the first time since my search began, I realized I was at a spot where I had found a clear path, and a guide to lead me down it. I wasn't alone anymore.

We arranged with the pastor of Queen of Peace to meet on Wednesday mornings, when Lotus went to a Bible-study class with my mother-in-law, so we could discuss matters of faith when the rambunctious three-year-old was elsewhere.

The meetings quickly fell into a comfortable pattern. Father would ask us what questions we had about the Faith, we would pose them, and he'd answer them as best he could. How does this conversion thing work, exactly? Was our marriage recognized, or did we have to do something to it? What is this Purgatory thing I keep hearing about, and does it mean I'm going to burn when I die, even if I'm not in Hell?

After that, Ken and I ran out of questions, since our ignorance about the Faith was that profound. I found the annoyingly named, but profoundly helpful *Catholicism for Dummies* and paired it with my brand-new copy of *The Catechism of the Catholic Church* and started from there. As I came across questions, I wrote them down and we asked Father.

I am so grateful to that priest for taking time out of his exhausting schedule to tailor classes for Ken and me. However, I began to notice flickers of ... *something* ... hovering around the periphery of our conversations.

The first indication came one Wednesday when Lotus's Bible-study class was cancelled. It was the first time we brought both kids with us to our weekly meeting, and Father smiled as he greeted four-month-old Joaquin again and met three-year-old Lotus for the first time.

He made some comment, some cryptic statement that I can't remember exactly, since it was so foreign to me at the time, about how beautiful our children were and how any future children were bound to be as cute. I looked at him, then at my kids, my girl and my boy, my matching set, then back at the priest, uncomprehending.

I think I incredulously said something along the lines of "More? Oh no!" and he immediately demurred with a bland, "Well, you're still young."

The exchange baffled me. Not out of any hostility toward children, exactly, but more out of a sense of "I have one of each, why would I have more?" I honestly couldn't understand what the point of more kids would be.

I knew the Church said no to birth-control pills and condoms and such, but since the psychotic reaction I had had to birth-control pills in the early days of our marriage, I had never used them since, and so the prohibition didn't show much on my radar. We had found other ways to avoid conceiving more kids, and so I hadn't given the matter much thought. But with the priest's mysterious comment, I began to realize that there was a whole area of Catholic teaching that we weren't covering in our self-directed meetings — an area that might possibly be a deal breaker. So all of us were reluctant to address it.

I started obsessing about sex (heh) and all the other "uncomfortable" aspects of Catholicism. I read what the *Catechism* had to say about it. I read what *Catholicism for Dummies* had to say about it. I started reading Catholic apologetics websites and spent way too much time on Catholic Answers. I couldn't help it. It was as if I had fallen down a rabbit hole, and it had opened into a world almost unbearable in its beauty.

I grew up and came of age in a pornography-soaked culture. I had learned to internalize the lie that sex was a consumable commodity, an activity on sale like any other aspect of human existence. I had bought into the associated lie that religion, in particular the Catholic Church, was a repressive, oppressive force against human sexuality, designed to make people feel shame and guilt about their bodies. So when I started delving into Church teachings on the divine gift of human sexuality, about the dignity and importance that it was imbued with, I was crushed. I was crushed by the weight of this new understanding in light of my prior actions and simultaneously freed by the promise of a more sublime future. All my life I'd thought sex to be little more than a collision of meat, and suddenly, I was being taught that it was a transcendent experience, designed to allow humanity to take part in divine creation and bring the participants closer together. This was not the actions of mere meat—this was a fusion of soul and body.

It was, simply and inadequately put, a revelation. And instead of making me turn tail and run, it brought me closer to the Church. If Catholicism could speak so counterculturally and so convincingly about sex, I wondered, what other truth bombs did it have in store for me?

While I was still unnerved by the prospect of a giant family where I became a Pez dispenser of baby after baby, I was both shocked and soothed by what I found out. I wanted to learn more. However, there was no way I was going to look our kindly, elderly priest in the eye and ask him to discuss sex with us, so it was back to online research for me, for the time being.

Finally at Rest

From this point, the eight months that must pass before I could be confirmed as a Catholic passed at the speed of light and slower than could be endured, simultaneously.

I had to track down both Ken's and my baptismal certificates, which meant I had to make a trip up to Michigan for one of them, since the church refused to mail me a copy. I had been baptized as an infant in a Congregational church that had since folded into another church. Ken had been baptized as a teen, at the Presbyterian church where we had met and been married.

I walked into that church with my mom for the first time since the wedding. The pastor had changed in the five years since we had left, and the new one was a stranger to both my mom and me.

"Now, what are you here for again?" he asked me. I had called earlier that day, spoken to a secretary, and was told to come up to the church at this specific time. The pastor was tall, big-boned, with snow-white hair, carefully combed back from his forehead. He was dressed in a white button-down shirt and black pants, and, despite the chill in the air, was sweating profusely.

"I need a copy of my husband's baptismal certificate," I said, feeling claustrophobic in the cluttered office. The man looked down at me, taking off his glasses, furrowing his brow. I began to feel the first twinge of fight-or-flight response.

"For what?" he asked, and I found myself actually biting my tongue in response to his tone.

"My husband and I are converting, and we need copies of our baptismal certificates." I tried to keep my voice steady and not defensive.

"Converting? To what?"

I debated my answer briefly. "Catholicism," I said, as he heaved a heavy sigh. He stared at me for a moment longer, then shrugged, and turned to a wall full of green books.

"Do you know what year? It'll take a minute to find it, but if you know the year ..."

Ten minutes later, my mom and I left the office with a baptismal certificate in hand while the pastor stood at the office window, watching us leave.

A Run Changes My (Pro-)Life

The Easter Vigil crept ever closer. All the paperwork was done, but there was still a giant, white elephant in the room I needed to address.

I knew, with every single cell in my body, that I could not join the Church and receive the Communion I was so longing for, unless I were *in* communion with the Church. The Eucharist was not a sign of "working toward unity," as it had been in the Protestant theology of my past. It is the fruit of a unity already established. When I stood in front of the parish at the Vigil Mass, I would be professing in words that I believed "all that the holy Catholic Church believes, teaches, and proclaims to be revealed by God." Consuming my First Holy Communion would be the profession of my body.

There was no way I could stand in front of God and lie to Him with my body. I might as well walk away and find a Protestant church whose teachings I approved of.

For the most part, this wasn't a problem. The logic and constancy I found in the Church's teaching drew me to it, even in areas I rebelled against at first, such as an all-male priesthood and the prohibition against contraception. Each time I questioned a Church teaching, as long as my questions were honest inquiries and not defensive posturing, the answer I got was clear, rational, and pointed toward a respect for human dignity that was shocking.

The last obstacle between me and the Church was abortion. Why wasn't "personally opposed but ..." good enough? Why did the Church insist that I make a universal stand against abortion?

My parents instilled certain values in me. This is what conscientious parents do. People who claim that passing along religious, political, or moral viewpoints to children is "mindless indoctrination" are either not parents or else parents who aren't thinking about what they're saying. So I'll say it here: The world is not going to hold back from promoting its religion, politics, morals, or ethics to your child, so why should you? By saying, "Let the child choose for himself," you're really saying, "Let the culture consume this child," because that's what's going to happen.

The values of my youth included such things as: the efficacy and necessity of labor unions, a strong and honest work ethic, the artistic genius of British comedy, and support for abortion. In our house, a woman's "right" to "control her body" was a nonissue. In fact, unlike labor unions and the primacy of British comedy, the possibility that there *was* an alternative to a pro-abortion stance wasn't even discussed.

So, when the time came for me to reexamine the values of my childhood, there were a number of things in the way of an honest critique of abortion.

Lack of opposing viewpoints. I don't think I encountered anyone who identified himself as anti-abortion until I was in high school, and then it was only one person. There may have been more of my peers who were pro-life, but none that I knew about. I more or less lived in an echo chamber, as far as life issues were concerned.

A wacky image. Anti-abortion activists were painted as religious crazies who were tools of the patriarchy and wanted to control every aspect of women's private lives. This was before the Internet, so it was easy to portray them this way. Today, with so many fantastic organizations able to circumvent traditional media outlets, anti-abortion activists can take control of their own image and help people realize that "anti-abortion" does not equal "spittle-flecked looney trying to bomb the local Planned Parenthood."

Contraceptive culture. Like almost every other person brought up in a post-Pill world, the thought that sex wasn't primarily for pleasure was foreign to me. With seemingly endless birth-control choices at our fingertips, if a human being were so rude as to get conceived at the wrong time in a woman's life, abortion seemed the obvious way to restore justice and sanity to a suddenly unjust and insane world.

Lack of experience; poor understanding of human development. Again, before the advent of the Internet as we know it, images of fetal development were not as easy to come by as they are now. Right this second, in the privacy of my own home, I can run a Google search and come up with hundreds of pictures of human life in all stages of development, learn that the heart begins beating at twenty-one days, and that from the moment of conception, a set of DNA, entirely distinct from either the sperm cell or the egg cell is present. It's a lot harder now to maintain the "fetus as a parasite/clump of cells/tumor/etc." fiction than it used to be.

So, for most of my life, my pro-abortion views went pretty much unchallenged. And then, two things happened.

The first was when a friend of mine told me about an abortion she had had. She doubtless wasn't my only friend who had had one, but she was the first who ever discussed it with me. Over drinks at a restaurant, she couldn't stop crying over something that she had chosen to do with her body to a clump of cells over ten years before. I remember my heart breaking for her—not because she had had an abortion, but because she was still so obviously shaken and sad about it. I remember thinking that I could have just as easily been in her shoes. I was sexually active before marriage; had I gotten pregnant at that time, I don't know if I would have viewed my options differently from the way she had viewed hers. So while I understood that she was sad and hurting, I honestly couldn't understand why. She had looked at her options, selected abortion as the best one for her, and exercised her choice. This was all in the pro-choice playbook—except the lingering emotional response. That was not something I remembered hearing in discussions about "a woman's reproductive choice."

I don't remember what I said to her. I pray that even then, while I was still in a spiritual wilderness, the Holy Spirit worked through me to bring the light of Christ to her. I don't know, though.

The second thing that happened was that I got pregnant with Lotus. For the first time in my life, I had a front-row seat at the whole spectacle of human development. I saw the gray, peanut-shaped little being floating in my uterus at nine weeks. I saw the little cursor-light of a heart flash on and off. And while that first ultrasound did not grant me the mystical bond with my baby that I had hoped for, it still made it shockingly clear that there was someone else in there. Not a tumor. Not a clump of cells. It was another human life. No longer was it just *my* body occupying that space.

This moved me from unexamined support for abortion to the lukewarm, "personally opposed, but ..." camp. Now I knew that *I* could never have an abortion, but I certainly wasn't going to tell someone else what to do. It seemed like a safe compromise on a hot-button topic. I could condemn it silently, but not have to mark myself as an object for scorn by making a universal condemnation of it.

Running Home

This was what I was grappling with one beautifully sunny October morning as I laced up my shoes and got ready for a run.

The Disney marathon was three months away, and Ken and I had worked out a nice training schedule. It was my morning to train, and I had a good eight miles ahead of me. Eight miles at the slow pace I run meant I had a solid hour and a half to fill with the sort of thoughts you use to distract yourself from the insanity of eight-mile runs.

I knew as I trotted off down the street that my constant companion for the next eight miles would be this issue of personally pro-life vs. universally pro-life. I had been round and round with myself on this topic for months, and I couldn't see any new way of looking at it. Then, as I rounded the first corner of my run and started up the first hill, I managed this small, inelegant prayer, "God, You've brought me this far. You know what I'm wrestling with here. I trust that You've brought me this close to the Catholic Church for a reason. I don't understand why abortion is always wrong, in every case, so I can't give You my understanding. But I do give You my trust and my obedience. Maybe it's enough that You know it's always wrong, and it's enough that I trust that."

And for a few moments, my soul was at peace. My mind was at peace. There was just the motion of my legs, and the rhythm of my breathing, and the giant flocks of blackbirds whirling overhead.

Then, softly, gently, I could feel a series of questions rising in my mind, like the first rays of the sun coming over the horizon. The questions centered on my realization that I would never choose to have an abortion. Realizing that I was engaged in a form of deep prayer with God, and He could see my heart more clearly than I ever could, I knew it would be foolish to be coy in my answers. I would never choose to have an abortion because I understood it to be the taking of another human being's life.

From that admission, the questions continued, gently, so gently that I knew they came from outside myself, as my internal voice is often very harsh and impatient. As I answered each question honestly, I could feel a sense of courage building within me. My obedience to God, even in an area I didn't entirely agree with, followed by my honesty in answering the tough questions resulted in an influx of supernatural courage that I needed to admit that I was, in fact, no longer pro-choice. And the fact that I no longer could support the only "choice" that was implied by that label meant that I was now pro-life.

Pro-life. I mulled that phrase over in my head a little bit and was shocked to discover that I was okay with it. The feelings of revulsion and near-hysterical rejection I usually experienced when running into anti-abortion people, laws, and philosophies were completely gone, replaced with a deep sense of peace and happiness.

Once again, I was faced with absolute proof that God is a gentleman who values our free will so much that He would never force us to do anything. It wasn't until I had given God my obedience in this area of Church teaching that He flooded my heart with the graces necessary to understand it. Anything else would have been a violation of my free will. But once I indicated with that act of will that I was open to His word, He moved me a million miles closer to Him in the course of a single run.

Easter Vigil

As friends and family learned about Ken's and my decision to become Catholic, the overwhelming response was one of puzzlement. They had trouble reconciling the New Age devotee who had been voted "Class Liberator" in high school with this woman who would go on and on about the early Church Fathers if given half a chance.

Eventually, all the paperwork was done, the weekly meetings finished, the news broken, and the Easter Vigil upon us. We made arrangements with the neighbors to watch Lotus and Joaquin, since the Vigil Mass didn't even start until past their bedtime and neither of us was particularly eager to wrestle with two cranky babies during a two-hour Mass.

We drove to the church in nervous silence. My sponsor was going to be there, but Ken's couldn't make it, so a proxy had been found for him.

My sponsor met us in the lobby. She smiled hugely when she saw us. "This is your First Holy Communion!" she said, and I nodded dumbly. I was thankful I had had ample time to recover from my first confession, which was as humbling and overwhelming an affair as can be imagined. I sincerely hoped that the Father would pretend he didn't remember the laundry list of sins I had confessed the week before.

We sat down, and I grabbed Ken's hand. It was only mid-April, but the air conditioners were already being pressed into service to cool the building, a task they did poorly. Or maybe they were working just fine, and it was just nerves making me sweat. Either way, Ken pulled his hand away from mine, and then made a big show of wiping the sweat off on my leg. I stuck my tongue out at him in return—but reverently, since we were in front of the Blessed Sacrament.

The night was a soft, impressionist painting of candlelight, incense, and warmth. I remember walking up to receive the Eucharist for the first time but don't remember consuming it.

I remember having a red felt stole placed around my shoulders at some point and standing side by side with my husband. I remember thinking that this whole moment was too big for me to take in all at once. I remember feeling overwhelmingly happy and peaceful.

After the vigil Mass was over and we had driven back home, we walked slowly across the cul-de-sac to gather our babies from the neighbors. We still had our felt stoles on, wearing them proudly despite the fact that they really were a bit tacky. The air was sweet and soft on my skin, and when Ken went to hold my hand, he didn't pull away because of the sweat factor.

Everyone knows that the secret to a happy ending is just knowing when to stop telling the story, and that moment, standing in the middle of the street with my beloved, would have been a great spot. But God wasn't done with me yet.

6

∾

Homeschool?

Two months after entering the Church, we had Lotus and Joaquin baptized—this time, done with proper Trinitarian formula and featuring exactly zero lakes. The days went on as they had—Ken still worked fourteen-hour days, six days a week. I still maintained a schedule to help fill my time, but at night, when I used to head up to the computer room to find God on the Internet, I now said a daily Rosary.

One of those nights, after the Rosary, I sat in the living room, listening to the air conditioner struggling to keep the house below 80 degrees. July in Mississippi is like living in a jungle. It would be months before the heat broke. The kids starting school in August would be going into buildings that were humid and sticky, despite the central air.

School.

Lotus had just turned four, and in the timeline I hadn't thought to question yet, four-year-olds unfailingly started pre-K. This was how it was done. If you were going to make education a priority, you had to start young. After all, you wouldn't want all that brainpower to be squandered. There were things to consider! Reading skills to master! A second language to conquer! Lotus's fourth year was slipping by and—oh my gosh, what if she didn't learn two-digit addition with one carry by then? Clearly, her life would be ruined.

A day later, I brought up the subject with Ken. He shrugged and asked me what I thought, since I was the "expert." I snorted. "Some expert," I said. If we went with my "expert" experience in public school, I'd never let her go. The things that I saw in my seven years of teaching at an award-winning school in an affluent suburban area of Michigan were enough to send me screaming for the hills. I couldn't imagine that a rural Mississippi school would offer anything better.

Despite some darker suspicions to the contrary, people do not go into education for the good benefits and summers off. Well, those who do don't stay long. The people I had the privilege of teaching alongside were some of the most generous and hardworking I've ever met. My hesitation to send Lotus to public school was not based on the caliber of the teachers. It stemmed from the very nature of conventional education.

One year, before my first-hour class, I had to find a way to single-handedly translate lesson plans into four languages. Four. That year, I had English-as-a-Second-Language students from Albania, China, Russia, and Mexico. None of them spoke more than a few words of English, and the mainstreaming policy of public schools meant that while they were provided English "acquisition" classes, they were still required to attend "English" classes, which are two very different things.

Using Babelfish, I hastily ran translations for "Identify the parenthetical phrase" in almost half a dozen languages. It was a farce. The kids were confused, I was confused, and while we tried to cobble together some emergency pidgin, the rest of the class grew bored and unsettled. I did, however, learn to say, "This is stupid" in multiple languages.

Homeschool?

Then there was the day when, in the middle of class, a new student was ushered into my room. I had to stop everything to greet him, fill out paperwork, and find him a seat. Then, as I paused to find where I had left off, the new boy—who was about fourteen—raised his hand. I called on him.

He gestured to my chest and asked, "Are those real?"

After he was ushered out of the classroom, I met with the principal, who had a helpless expression on his face. The student, he explained, was clinically diagnosed with something called Oppositional Defiant Disorder.

"Part of the manifestation of this disorder is deliberately seeking to annoy others, volatile anger, and a marked disregard for authority. We can't suspend him for saying that to you. It wouldn't do any good. Not only is this behavior part of his disability; the child would just sit at home unattended, and we'd lose him for sure ... Maybe if he writes you an apology?"

I stared at the principal.

The teachers I worked with made heroic efforts to show their students that public school didn't have to be like this. But it so often felt like a losing battle, and I didn't want to toss my daughter into it.

One of the nearby parishes had a school that offered pre-K classes. A private Catholic school seemed like a better option, or at least one I wasn't intimately familiar with. Ken and I went to tour the facilities. We walked into the school and were greeted by a seven-foot statue of Our Lady of the Immaculate Conception, and I reached for my Miraculous Medal absently. I felt so agitated, so anxious during the tour, that not even seeing Mary standing guard over the hallways comforted me.

After the tour, Ken and I sat in the director's office and numbly signed some papers. Ken's numbness was in response to the tuition. Mine was at the prospect of sending Lotus away from the family five days a week, for six hours at a time. It seemed wrong. Too much. Too soon.

For the next week, every time Ken got home in the early hours of the morning, he'd find me crying. That ugly, four-in-the-morning-crying-in-the-dark kind of crying that never means good things for anyone. The first couple of days, he tried to ask me what was wrong, and I tried to hide it from him.

Finally, it got too much for me, and I admitted that I couldn't stand the thought of sending Lotus away to school. He stood there in the dark, and I could barely make out his shape, standing motionless for a few moments.

Then came the voice of common sense that I couldn't find on my own: "Don't send her. Homeschool her."

Homeschool her? *Homeschool* her? The thought had never crossed my mind. In my time as a public school teacher I had run across exactly two homeschoolers. One had not actually been educated at home, but was instead pressed into service as a care provider for her younger siblings. When she came to me, she was in seventh grade and unable to read. She would spend the school day with her forehead on her desk, rocking from side to side. The other homeschooler was possibly the smartest individual in that building, but had such a repugnant personality that no one could bear speaking to him to find out for sure.

And yet ... I couldn't get the idea out of my head. It was with something close to glee that I went back to my late-night Internet searches.

Ken and I decided to give homeschooling a year's trial. I found a provider of Catholic curricula, bought lesson plans and reading programs and math manipulatives and Latin readers and CDs with Gregorian chant and possibly quite a few other things I didn't need and would end up not using. Then I set out to find a support group.

The only problem was, well, location. There I was in Mississippi, the heart of the Bible Belt, surrounded by people who, at best, tended to view Catholics as misguided, and at worst believed us to be the anti-Christ. There was a large homeschool presence in the Memphis area, but the ones I knew about required families to sign "Statements of Faith," which unfailingly professed belief in Protestant-only ideas like *sola Scriptura* and salvation by faith alone.

I dejectedly scrolled through page after page. Maybe there was a secular group that wouldn't be too antagonistic to religion. Then something caught my eye. It was a picture of Our Lady bending over the Infant Jesus, with the title "Blessed Sacrament Homeschool Group."

Picture of Mary? Blessed Sacrament? Things don't get much more Catholic than that. I quickly scrolled through their website and sent a breathless e-mail to the membership liaison.

Like all things in life, there was no way I could have known it at the time, but between the decision to try homeschooling and the e-mail I had just sent, my life was about to get bigger, better, and crazier.

I Meet My Best Friend

A few days later, the phone rang with caller ID showing a local number and name I didn't recognize. In violation of my normal "avoid the phone at all costs" mentality, I answered it. I hate phone conversations.

The woman at the other end introduced herself as Kim, from the homeschool group. I was feeling very awkward and self-conscious, but thankfully, Kim had done this before, and

I didn't have to say much. While she talked about the group, about the sorts of activities it offered, I nodded my head, listening to the sounds behind her words—the sounds of children running and laughing and arguing and crashing into things. One crash was particularly loud, and Kim paused for a second, a muffled admonishment was delivered, and then she picked up her sentence right where she'd left off.

Where I would have felt the need to explain and justify the interruption, Kim didn't. She continued on as if nothing unusual had happened, and I was in awe of her mothering confidence.

We chatted a bit about curriculum choices, pre-K expectations, and tips for starting homeschool. Then she invited me over to her house that Friday for a playdate she hosted every week for the group.

"That sounds great!" I said, reeling at the possibility of spending time with another adult during the day.

"Okay, good! Now, I have to tell you, there will be lots of kids at the playdate. Lots of kids, and we're not the type of group to hover over the kids at all times. So, just to prepare you before you come over . . ." she trailed off.

I nodded. "The more, the merrier, right?"

"Yeah," Kim said, "but like, *lots* of kids. Like, I'm pregnant right now with my tenth."

I paused for a moment, trying to process this. Her . . . tenth? In my entire life, I had never met anyone who had more than six children, with the sole exception of a boy I went to high school with, who was rumored to be one of fourteen, but this had never been proven. I realized I had let the silence extend too long and hastily tried to remedy it.

"Wow! Great! Ten kids! Okay, we'll be there on Friday!" Kim's voice sounded wryly amused as she gave me her address and we hung up. I stood there for a moment with the phone still in my hand, astounded. Ten kids. Was this my future?

Despite my fears about becoming Old Mother Hubbard, I was looking forward to the playdate. Friday came, and I loaded up Lotus and Joaquin, and headed down the road to Kim's house, unable to imagine what would be waiting for me.

The house was on a cul-de-sac, and there were cars parked everywhere. I could have picked which house was Kim's without being told: it was the one that had about eight kids in the front yard, with ages ranging from fourteen down to three or four. The thing I noted instantly was all the kids seemed to be hanging out with each other regardless of age. Older kids pushed younger kids on bikes while carrying on intense conversations with other big kids; middle kids had sword fights with sticks, while others pretended to be dragons breathing fire on the sword fighters. The kids all waved to the three of us as we walked up the path, and a boy who looked about thirteen pointed me in the direction of a side door.

"The front door is locked. Go in the side!" he said cheerfully, then turned back to a tall, blonde girl he had been talking to, while absently swinging a toddler from his arms.

I knocked as directed, and a dark-haired girl answered. She had a sweet face and earnest, sincere eyes.

"Hi!" she said, as five or six boys wrestled on the couches behind her. "Are you here for playdate? Are these your kids? Are there more? I'm Faith. Who are you?"

Before I could answer, Lotus introduced herself and grabbed Faith's hand, and the two of them ran upstairs where the other girls were gathered.

I wandered stupidly through the house, until a grownup spotted me. She had pale red hair, skin the color of milk, and was gloriously pregnant. She had a glass of tea in her hand and a smile on her face.

"I'm Kim," she said motioning me to follow her, "You must be Cari. I'm glad you could make it. Come on in, and I'll introduce you to the other moms."

I followed her into a red-paneled dining room, which was dominated by the largest table I had ever seen outside a cafeteria. Seated around that mammoth table were five or six other women. The table was covered with food and drinks, the women were laughing about something, and everyone sat easily, obviously comfortable with themselves and with each other.

Walking into a situation like that as the outsider is the stuff that middle-school nightmares are made of. Yet when all the women turned to look at me while Kim made introductions, I didn't feel I was being scrutinized—just welcomed. When one of them offered me a glass of Coke and some Cheetos, I knew I was in the right place.

Nodding hellos to each woman, I pulled up a chair and sat down at a table that would become, outside the Sacraments, the most grace-filled part of my life. I wish that every person will at some point be blessed with a community, a pack of friends like the ones I made at Kim's table.

Week after week we'd meet while our massive child army whooped and hollered and squeezed every drop out of their childhood. We laughed until we cried, cried until we laughed, and puzzled out all the mysteries and traps of marriage and motherhood. Women would come and go and come back and leave again, and the cast of characters on those Friday playdates was as fluid as water. But the thing that was constant was the honest desire to help build each other's faith and family.

Homeschool?

For instance, for me, time spent with those women filled in the gaps of my RCIA experience. I learned about Natural Family Planning, the different methods, the different reasons for using it or discarding it. Around Kim's table, I learned to stop clenching my fists in anticipation of what would happen if I opened wide and let God work in my soul. I learned the primal, simple secret that our culture has murdered: children are a blessing, and being open to the possibility of new life means you will be rewarded with a more fertile life in the broadest sense of the word.

And as if that weren't enough, as if God hadn't already heaped the blessings on me in a landslide, I found in Kim a kindred spirit. She was funny, humble, quick-witted, and an example of a woman trying her hardest to live life for God. All that and more, wrapped up in a redheaded spitfire personality.

I may have found my way to Catholicism on my own, during long, solitary nights tracking down God on the Internet, but at Kim's table I learned to live out that faith as part of a universal family, one Friday playdate at a time.

Time Passes

Those first couple of years in Mississippi had been in many ways a very lonely time for me. Making the transition from working mom to stay-at-home mom was so much more difficult than I had ever imagined. It wasn't just the externals, such as how to spend our time or what routines and schedules to set up. There was also a massive shift required in how I saw myself.

Throughout my childhood, the question was never, "Are you going to college?" but rather, "Where are you going to college?" My mom worked outside the home, as did both my grandmothers, even in postwar years. So valuable to them was the concept of paid labor that I was confused and ashamed of my desire to leave my career behind and stay home with my children.

I had worked hard to become a teacher. I had gotten a job in an affluent school district, in a brand-new building, and worked hard to earn my Masters degree. I enjoyed teaching. I was good at it.

But I wanted to give it all up for my kids.

In Mississippi, I learned to stop viewing my new life as a cop-out. I had to stop feeling as if my work didn't matter because it didn't pay cash. I had to stop feeling guilty and start being happy that I was given a chance to be with my babies.

I fumbled my way through this mostly by myself. Until I found Kim and the homeschool group, I hadn't made many friends.

Those first two years, Ken left for work shortly before most people's working days ended, and he didn't get home until a few hours before most people get up in the morning. This meant that the ordinary activities moms with young children do together, such as meeting at the park or going to the zoo, took place when our family was busy spending time together — since Ken was awake and not at work.

Evenings were no better. As the only parent home, I couldn't go meet other moms without getting a sitter, a luxury we couldn't afford. It was lonely. At the time, I didn't realize how difficult it was, and I'm grateful that I didn't.

But it didn't stay like that. Ken's Saturday shifts ended, and his days went from fourteen hours to a more manageable eleven or twelve. He still worked second shift, which made outings with other people difficult to arrange, but with the discovery of Friday playdates at Kim's house, I got some regular grown-up time. Kim's oldest daughter became our trusted family babysitter.

Homeschool?

The exposure to large families that we were getting through the homeschool group was like being welcomed into an exotic, wild country we had never imagined existed. Soon, Ken and I started talking about having another baby. Honestly, even *contemplating* moving from a two-and-done, a-boy-and-a-girl mentality to seeing children as a natural part of marriage, was a bigger shift than deciding to have kids at all.

So, with hands wide open, rather than clenched into fists of fear, we conceived our third child. I marked off the forty weeks of pregnancy at Kim's table, sitting and laughing with my friends, cracking up as each week I had to push my chair farther and farther back to accommodate my rapidly growing belly.

Doctor Black and Shirley

For insurance reasons, I wasn't able to use my beloved Doc Ostrich Boots for this next baby's birth. I suffered a long, horrible moment of panic. I had wild thoughts of giving birth in the backyard solo, squatting just out of the range of the porch light so the June bugs wouldn't fly into me. After all, if Doc Ostrich Boots couldn't deliver my child, whom could I trust?

I posed this question one Friday at playdate.

"Doctor Black" came the immediate answer in unison from four women.

"Doctor Black's delivered six of my babies," said one, "and he never gives me a hassle about having a large family."

"He's pro-life. Won't perform abortions," said another.

"Well, he prescribes birth control if pressed, but it's for licensing reasons, and he'll tell you it has abortifacent properties and then give you the number for NFP coaches in the area," came another voice.

"He used to be Catholic, but he left the Church and is Baptist now," said Kim, and there was a long moment of silence from the table, as if the group were collectively mourning the loss of such a great doctor.

"And don't forget Shirley!" someone blurted out. The moment of silence was broken by a wall of laughter.

Doctor Black certainly seemed like a better alternative than the backyard with the June bugs, so the following Monday I called his office. A lady with a thick southern accent answered the phone.

"Doctor Black's office. Can I help you?" her voice, while thick with drawl, somehow had a clipped quality when it said, "Can I help you?" that made me suspect the speaker wasn't really interested in whether she could help or not.

"Yes. I was calling to see if Doctor Black was accepting new patients?" There was a mighty sigh heaved at the other end, followed by a long silence.

"Um ... hello?" I asked, wondering whether we had been disconnected.

"Honey, I'm still here." I've never heard the word *honey*, spoken in a Southern accent, sound so hostile. I felt a little twinge of fear stir in my heart. "I'm just looking at my calendar. Now, when was your last period?" I opened my mouth then shut it. Then opened it again and shut it again. I was confused.

"Um ... my last ...? So, he *is* taking new patients?"

The same sigh again. "Honey, I need to know when you're due before I can tell you if he can take you. He's all booked up for December, March, and May, so if you're due then, he can't take you. So, when was your last period?"

I told her, there was more silence as calculations were made, then the speaker came back. "Well, that makes your due date

Homeschool?

June 17. Which is fine, because the doctor doesn't have too many other babies that month. You can come in two weeks. Bring your driver's license and your insurance card." I heard a click, and we were disconnected. I slowly put the phone down on the counter and wondered what I was getting into.

Two weeks later, I parked my car in front of a very confusing building and tried to find my way to Dr. Black's office. After three misfires, I stumbled upon the right one and approached the check-in desk.

A sliding window of hazy Plexiglas separated me from the woman behind the counter. She was on the phone, and I immediately recognized her voice as the woman I had spoken with. She wore a white cardigan over faded pink-and-blue scrubs, had wire-rimmed glasses perched on the end of her nose, and her smooth black skin made her age hard to judge. Somewhere between thirty-five and ninety was my best guess.

She hung up the phone and turned her attention to paperwork on her desk. I cleared my throat awkwardly and put my purse on the desk, just to make sure she saw me.

If she did, she made no indication. She just kept shuffling papers around.

"Excuse me, I'm here for a —"

The woman held up an index finger at me, still without making eye contact. I looked around the office stupidly, certain that this was some sort of mistake. This was the office all my friends raved about? *This?*

Then I remembered: "Don't forget Shirley!" This must be Shirley.

Finally, Potential Shirley flung aside the Plexiglas window. "Name?" she said, looking at me from over the tops of her glasses.

"Cari Donaldson," I said, amused at the intimidation I felt about her.

"Mmm-hmmm," Potential Shirley said. "You're late."

"I couldn't find the right office ...? I walked into a couple others by mistake." Shirley looked at me over the tops of her glasses so dramatically that her chin buried itself in her extremely large chest. Her gaze ran up then down me, her eyebrows raised in a skeptical angle.

"Mmm-hmmmm," she finally said, as if she'd acquired some disappointing information about me in her scan. "Fill out this paperwork. And remember, honey, we're the office with the big red lab box on the outside." She slammed the Plexiglas window shut and had clearly removed me from her memory before I had even returned to my seat.

When I eventually got in to meet Doctor Black, I realized that he was the perfect complement to Potential Shirley. He was extremely tall, extremely pale, and with a manner that reminded me of Droopy Dog from the old cartoons. His drawl was charming, his personality low-key, and, most importantly, he sat down on a stool and asked me if I had any questions for him. Anyone who has ever had a doctor who glances impatiently at his watch in response to a question knows what an amazing thing it is to have a doctor who sits first and *then* checks to see if you have questions.

Doctor Black was like the placid country doctor you see in movies. Nothing ruffled his feathers, and it seemed nothing surprised him. On the other hand, his mild manner made it easy to underestimate him. Nothing escaped his attention.

I found this out months later, when Doctor Black picked up an anomaly in the baby's heartbeat from a fifteen-second observation. His normally relaxed face furrowed into a frown, his eyes squinted, and the whole "semi-bumbling country doctor" aura slipped away. He sent me to the hospital for an extended ultrasound. We discovered that everything was fine, but the baby's umbilical cord was wrapped around his neck.

By the time the results from the ultrasound were in, easygoing Doctor Black was back, and he looked over my chart in calm satisfaction. The baby was fine, the heart was fine, and even the cord around the neck was "nothing worrisome," which did little to calm me, although I tried to be calm. Shirley put everything into perspective as I walked up to the Plexiglas window to schedule my next appointment.

She slowly slid the window open, while staring at my chart over the tops of her glasses. One eyebrow rose, and she looked at me.

"Says here that you need to come back in a week," she accused, looking at me as if I were trying to pull a fast one on her.

"Yes, ma'am," I said. "The cord is wrapped around the baby's neck. I think the doctor wants to just keep a close eye on things." This news was met with a snort from Shirley.

"Well, honey, don't let that worry you none. It's not like that baby's breathing in there yet."

With that sage advice echoing in my head, I bemusedly left Doctor Black's office.

Getting to Work

Having a third child is a tipping point in a family. There are tactical considerations, of course—the arrival of Number Three means that the grownups are now outnumbered. In basketball terms, the adults are reduced to a Zone defense, rather than Man-on-Man. Then there are cultural considerations: for a large portion of my life, I assumed that if you had your boy and girl, you simply stopped having children. No need to "try for" a child of the missing sex. And for Ken and me, there were logistical considerations: having a third child meant that someone was going to have to Share a Room.

I never had to share a room growing up. Furthermore, I had seen enough sitcoms and heard enough horror stories from room-sharing friends to believe that sharing a room with a sibling was the worst thing that could ever happen to you. Then there was the infallible psychobabble doctrine that stated, "It's crucial for every human being to have his own personal space." It was this teaching that now made me seriously fear for my children's sanity if two of them had to split a bedroom.

All these anxieties came to a head one day late in my pregnancy when I was trying to maneuver my gigantic abdomen around the dryer to swap out a load of laundry. My kitchen was a disaster, Joaquin was wearing an extremely wet diaper and nothing else, and Lotus emerged from my bedroom, having apparently just cut some of her own hair. I surveyed my landscape and had a crippling moment of panic. A voice from somewhere said, *"This is what my life is going to be like for the next eighteen years."*

I couldn't breathe. I started to get tunnel vision. I had a brief, vivid image of myself, two decades from now, standing in the exact same spot, gripping the exact same load of laundry, while FEMA workers raided my house, having to clear a path using a bulldozer.

A frantic prayer was thrown up to God. A jumbled mess of a prayer, asking for a combination of courage, peace, humor, and a magical housekeeper descending from the sky on an umbrella.

Three out of four ain't bad. Immediately after I asked for divine help, a calm, reassuring sense of peace came over me. This

Homeschool?

was my life now. And although it didn't look or smell or sound like I thought it would, that wasn't cause for panic. This was a good life, given to me by a good God, and now it was time to stop stalling on that laundry and get to work.

So I did. Well, mostly. I still stalled on laundry,[12] but I got to work in other ways. I finished up our first year of homeschooling, which, since Lotus had learned to read during it, I counted as a success. I volunteered at our parish. I washed baby clothes and stored baby clothes and tried to prep Joaquin for the arrival of a younger sibling.

I even, completely out of the blue and with no advance warning whatsoever, found myself in the middle of a discussion about human reproduction with my four-year-old daughter one day.

We were in the car when her sweet little voice came from the backseat, "Mommy? How did the baby get inside you?"

Ken and I had already wisely and sensibly discussed how we would deal with questions regarding human sexuality—we would answer them honestly as they were posed, but not offer any additional information unless asked. There would be a time and place for the full story, so there was no need to rush.

All this was well and good, but we never thought to figure out what we'd say when the questions were asked.

Throwing a quick prayer in the general direction of the Holy Spirit, I answered her question honestly and at a level I figured a bright four-year-old could understand: "Daddy had a sperm cell and Mommy had an egg cell. The two cells met, and the baby started growing."

I could hear Ken start making strangled noises as soon as the word *sperm cell* was uttered. He fiddled with the radio to try to

---

[12] Who am I kidding? I don't do the laundry. Ken does.

turn it up. I glared an invitation for him to join in the conversation and stop letting me flounder alone.

He pretended not to see my glare.

The answer I had given seemed to satisfy Lotus, who offered no follow-up questions. She just thoughtfully repeated the words *sperm cell* and *egg cell* to herself for the rest of the way home. Ken pretended not to hear. I pretended not to wince.

Once the initial shock of impromptu sex talks was over, I felt very self-congratulatory.

Our daughter was clearly happy with the answer to her question, since she delighted in repeatedly telling Joaquin, "Mommy has a baby inside her. It got there because Daddy's sperm cell and her egg cell SMASHED! together, and BAM! a baby was started!" This story was always very animated and contained a loud handclap at "BAM!" Her brother never got tired of listening to it, and she never got tired of telling it. Clearly, this was because I was a mothering pro. Clearly I had laid the foundation for a lifetime of pro-life sentiment. Clearly people would start lining up at my door for pointers on how to broach the subject of sex in a way that was life affirming, awe-filled, and modest.

Then Halloween came.

I got the kids into their costumes, buckled Joaquin into his stroller, and off we went. We visited our neighbor across the street first—a kindly, elderly lady, who had flawless Southern manners and was aptly summed up in the word *refined*.

Lotus, who is nothing if not gregarious, charmed her way to three fun-size Snickers bars with her chatter. Our neighbor smiled indulgently as the four-year-old talked about her costume, her brother's costume, their candy, the weather, whatever. When she could finally get a word in edgewise, the neighbor asked in her slow drawl, "Well, dear, I hear that you're going to be a big sister again. How exciting. What do you think about all this?"

My daughter didn't even pause. She drew herself up straight, shook her little head like a mother hen, and said, "Well, I think that it's *very* interesting. You see, Daddy had a sperm cell, and Mommy had an egg cell—"

The world stopped. My mouth fell open in shock. I could feel my face burning hot and my heart start racing. Fight or flight, and my body was clearly trying to choose flight.

"... and they SMASHED! together, and BAM! my little brother was started!"

She smacked her hands together, finished her story, and looked at our elderly neighbor with a satisfied smile.

My neighbor looked at me, standing there on her driveway, while I was wishing for lightning to strike me dead.

Then she started to laugh. It built into huge, shoulder-shaking laughter. I managed a weak smile and looked around for a way to flee the scene.

"Oh, honey," she said to me, wiping her eyes and trying to catch her breath. "With a storyteller like that in your house, you need a beer. But I'm out, so I'm just going to give you some candy." And she pressed a couple of fun-size Snickers into my hands and waved us goodbye, still shaking her head with laughter as we faded (thankfully) into the night.

7

∞

Trial by Childbirth

I was in the home stretch of the pregnancy when Shirley gave voice to the thought no one else would.

Waddling into the office for my appointment one swelteringly hot day in early June, Shirley caught sight of me, slapped the Plexiglas window open before I had even crossed the office's threshold, and announced to the entire room, "Girl, is the doctor sure there's only one in there?"

No longer intimidated by Shirley and fueled by raging pregnancy hormones, I scowled at her in response. She laughed at my expression—deep, shoulder-shaking laughter. I would have bet a million dollars that she was actually slapping her knee under the desk in her mirth.

"Shirley. I don't even. I got pulled over and got a speeding ticket on the way here today. A ticket!" This just made her laugh harder, and she demanded I tell her the whole story about the meanest cop in Memphis—who, I explained, wouldn't let an obviously pregnant woman off with a warning, even though she pretended to have contractions during the encounter.

Now she was doubled over laughing. I wished I could take a video of her, since no one would ever believe me when I told them on Friday that I had made Shirley not only crack a smile, but also bust a gut. Someone walked into the office behind me, and Shirley immediately stopped laughing and slid the Plexiglas window shut in the woman's startled face. She turned to look at me in confusion.

I shrugged. "That's Shirley for you," I said, and took my seat.

Doctor Black echoed Shirley's observation, but far more gently.

"Well, this one looks like he's going to be a big 'un. But third children usually are. So let's talk about an induction." I rolled my eyes. Another induction.

Doctor Black chuckled. "Let's call the hospital and schedule it for two weeks. You'll probably go into labor before that on your own, but just in case ..."

Of course I didn't go into labor on my own. Two weeks passed with nothing but false alarms.

The induction was scheduled for June 18, but Ken thought it would be great if I went into labor on my own on June 17, which was Joaquin's birthday.

"The boys could share a birthday!" he said, as if this were a selling point.

I thought it was a terrible idea.

"Sharing a room is one thing," I said. "Sharing a birthday is something else entirely. Everyone deserves his own birthday. There's no way I'm going into labor on the 17th. If I have to, I'll cross my legs the whole day, and even if I have regular contractions, I'm not telling you until midnight."

He shook his head at me, I stuck my tongue out at him, and I made good on my promise. Joaquin's birthday came and went with not a single contraction detected.

My sister-in-law, her two girls, and my parents were all in town for Joaquin's birthday party, so they extended their stay a couple of days longer, and we made a merry little group at the hospital the next day.

Ken and I were shown to the labor room, while everyone else hunkered down for what turned out to be an extremely long wait. Doctor Black strolled in, attempted to break my water to start labor, and discovered that he couldn't.

He stood up, frowning slightly and sighing. "Well, that big baby of yours doesn't want to come out. Why don't you two go walk around the hospital for an hour. Maybe that'll bring him down far enough that I can rupture the membrane."

With that charming offer in mind, Ken and I set off to pace. And pace. And pace some more, much to the irritation of the janitor who was trying to buff the floors of the maternity wing.

Finally the good doctor was able to break my water, which barely started labor, which required more walking to make sure I stayed in labor. My mom came to walk me through the halls when Ken needed a break. My sister-in-law entertained four children who were increasingly desperate to meet this new baby—who was taking so long to appear that they began to doubt his very existence.

Every centimeter I dilated was a battle. At six centimeters I stalled out, and Doctor Black cheerfully strolled into the room, asked me if I wanted "a sniff of Pitocin to speed things along."

"NO!" I yelled at him, too irritated by my body and too scared of Pitocin to be polite. Doctor Black didn't mind. He smiled, shrugged his shoulders, and strolled out of the room, leaving me alone to labor in excruciatingly slow misery.

Lotus, Joaquin, and my two nieces made periodic visits to my room, until finally, thankfully, things progressed far enough down the pain trail that I couldn't have the kids with me anymore.

Finally, it was time to push. As slow as everything had been up to this point, the baby made up for it in the homestretch. He crowned briefly, then finally decided to make his appearance into the world with what I swore was an audible "Pop!"

My clearest memory from the pushing stage was thinking, "*Oh . . . Oh, that can't be good for me. There's no way that can be good.*"

But I didn't think about it for long, because another push, and out came beautiful, gigantic Gabriel. Gigantic Gabriel who was so seriously bruised from the exit from my body that his nose was squashed and his face was all purple. He proved Doctor Black's prediction correct—that the third child was the biggest. At nine pounds, seven ounces, he was a huge bundle of hungry and angry.

Ken looked down at Gabriel, who was wrapped in his arms like a fat burrito.

"It's all that Coke you've been drinking at Friday playdate," he accused. I just smiled and took Gabriel to nurse him.

"Fat babies are cute," I said absently.

Then the doors to the room burst open, and six people poured in to meet the newest member of the family.

Gabriel Cries. A lot.

For the next six months, if Gabriel wasn't nursing or sleeping, he was crying. He was the unhappiest baby I ever had. The only way I could keep him happy was if he was in the sling, strapped to my chest, and I was actively moving.

I remember one of the first days of school, two months after Gabriel's birth. Joaquin was at the table, eating Play-Doh, Lotus was next to him, and I was standing behind her, trying to help her with her math while swaying back and forth, desperately rocking Gabriel into silence. It looked very calm and under control, but on the inside, I was undone. I had opened myself to life, and now I felt like I was drowning.

A friend of mine, who was a chiropractor, offered to adjust him. She said often the cramped uterine conditions of their final months result in painful kinks in babies' spines, and an adjustment could offer some relief.

I gratefully took her up on her offer, and she had me sit cross-legged on the floor with the baby in my lap.

"Hold your arms straight out," she instructed. "I'm going to try and press your arms down, but you resist me, ok?" I looked at her funny. She caught my look and nodded.

"I know. It sounds kooky. But trust me." So trust her I did, and she placed one hand on my arm, the other on Gabriel's spine. She slowly moved her hand along his spine, pressing down on my arm from time to time. Then, she moved her hand to a spot on Gabriel's back, pressed down on my arm, and my arm inexplicably dipped under her gentle push.

"There it is," she said. She told me I could put my arms down.

Taking Gabriel from me, she pressed gently into a spot on his back, he stretched his neck up and to either side, grunted in satisfaction, and then drooled on her hand.

"That should do it," she said, handing him back to me. I stared at her, waiting for an explanation.

She looked sheepish. "Okay, it's going to sound strange. Like, voodoo-strange, and if I hadn't seen it with my own eyes, I wouldn't believe it myself." She stopped, embarrassed. I motioned her to continue.

"Well, there's a theory that mothers and babies are connected by an invisible umbilical cord. A sort of psychic link.

When I touched each spot on Gabriel's back, I pressed down on your arm. At each spot, you resisted my push. Then I got to this spot here," she said, pointing to a place on Gabriel's back. "That time, when I pushed, your arm moved. That's how I knew that was the spot giving the baby trouble."

I shook my head at her. "Voodoo," I said. She agreed.

But a few moments later, I steeled myself to load Gabriel into his car seat, an event that always resulted in screaming —screaming that would end only when I got home and took him out of his seat. Now, there was silence as I strapped him in. No crying.

I looked at my friend, and she looked at me. Gabriel sucked on his pacifier and looked at both of us calmly. No crying.

"Voodoo," we said in unison, and I hopped in the car and sped home before the voodoo could wear off and screaming Gabriel return.

The adjustment's magic eventually did wear off. Unhappy, crying Gabriel returned. For a time. Then it stopped. He was six months old, we were on our way to Mass, and Ken and I looked at each other, shocked. We had been having a normal conversation at a normal volume, and there hadn't been a baby wailing over it.

We parked the car, carefully removed the not-crying Gabriel from his seat, holding him like a bomb that could go off at any moment. We walked into church, a pretty little picture of a family of five, with zero screaming children among us.

For the first time in months, we risked sitting in the main part of church, rather than hiding in the soundproof "cry" room. As I knelt down to give thanks for the week, I glanced down the pew at my family. Five-year-old Lotus, kneeling and praying, her eyebrows knit together in concentration; two-year-old

Joaquin, pulling at the straps of his blue Crocs and trying to settle next to his Daddy; then my beautiful husband, made even more attractive with the addition of a calmly sleeping baby in his arms. I was flooded with gratitude to God for all the gifts He'd poured out on me.

It was an actual, physical response, and I found myself unclenching my fists and my heart and thinking, "Another child wouldn't be so bad, God."

That's all it took.

There Are No Atheists with Home Pregnancy Tests

I believe that every woman who has ever peed on a white plastic stick in the silence of her bathroom is, even if just for the tiniest flicker of a moment, united with all women in some sort of religious experience.

No matter what you want the result to be, or even if you're not sure what result you're hoping for, that moment of waiting, straining to see how many lines are going to rise to the surface, is accompanied by a prayer.

"Please. No."

"Please. Yes."

"Please."

Even if you're not entirely aware of the petition. Even if you're not sure whom you're throwing the desperate request at. That moment of waiting turns us all into spiritual beings, even for just a frantic, split second.

The first time I took a pregnancy test was when we were trying for Lotus. There was nothing accidental or unplanned about it. We had worked for the creation of this child with the single-minded focus that you only engage in with your first. Names were picked, birth plans crafted, parenting philosophies adopted—all before we'd even conceived a baby. But there was no way we were going to be unprepared.

No way.

As I sat there in my early-morning bathroom, holding the purple-and-white plastic stick, I was blindsided by the feeling of panic that suddenly overcame me. I was scared to turn the test over and read the results: if I didn't look, both results were still possible, so I could pretend that there *was* no result. But once I looked, well, I'd know.

I breathed out a tiny prayer that filled the whole bathroom with its sincerity and then flipped the test over in my hands.

Positive.

I stared at it for a long moment, and then said, "Well ... Well, there it is." I stood up, got ready for work, and passed the day in a pre–cell phone agony that I couldn't tell my husband that we were parents until we were both home from work.

He came home that evening to find the test kit tied up with a bow, sitting next to a bottle of sparkling apple juice. Even with all those props, he still didn't know how to decipher the message. I had to read it to him.

That was the last time I ever put a pregnancy test on display, but it wasn't the last time I found myself praying my way through the five-minutes-until-results waiting period. Countless plastic sticks have worked their chemistry magic in my bathrooms, and every one of them was accompanied by prayer.

Three weeks after that spontaneous prayer at Mass, I suspected I was pregnant with our fourth child. This time, I went the stingy route and bought an off-brand test to save a few dollars. I got home and began the familiar drill of unwrapping and peeing and waiting while Gabriel—fussy, irritable, six-months-old Gabriel—could be heard crying in his crib.

Trial by Childbirth

The multitude of prayers uttered while that test took its sweet, off-brand time to develop obviously didn't help the results, which were inconclusive. There was the faintest trace of a second line, suggesting pregnancy, but only if you held it just so against the light and didn't blink.

Angrily, I stomped out to the living room, and thrust the test at Ken. He took it, looked at it for a second, and looked at me blankly.

"What does it say?" he asked, handing the test back to me.

"I don't know!" I yelled, refusing to take back the stick. "Are there two lines? Or one? Is that a second line? Do you see it? Do you?" He looked at it again, turning it this way and that against the light. Finally he shrugged.

"I can never tell what these things say."

I muttered about off-brand tests, and he told me that in the morning we'd go spend the big bucks for a fancy, name-brand one, but until then, there was nothing I could do about it. Either I was or I wasn't. The test wouldn't change that.

Impeccable logic leaving me no room to argue, I spent the rest of the night in irritated, frantic prayer. I wanted another baby, but now that the possibility arose that this desire may have been manifested in reality, I found myself panicking about the timing. Three children under the age of six, and now there may be a *fourth* added to the mix? What were we *thinking*? Why would God *listen* to such an obviously reckless request? Eventually, my prayers shrank down to a two-word petition:

"God, please."

The next day, I bought the Cadillac of pregnancy tests. This thing was as big as a deck of cards and it spelled out the results out for you: "pregnant" or "not pregnant." No two lines, no mystery. I brought it home, took it, showed the results to Ken, and then stuffed the thing in my pocket to show to Kim, whose house we were going to for dinner that night.

Finding ourselves alone in the kitchen, I told Kim about my off-brand pregnancy fail, and how I had retested that morning. I pulled the test out of my pocket and showed it to her.

As she looked at it, I started crying. "What am I *doing*? What were we thinking? What was *God* thinking? Four kids under the age of seven? Three of them three and under? What am I going to *do*?"

Without hesitating for a second, she hugged me.

Handing me back the test, she said with absolute sincerity, "Congratulations! Babies are awesome; children are a blessing. God has blessed you, and you and Ken are fantastic parents."

Hearing those words, I realized that God *had* answered those frantic pretest prayers of mine. He responded to my "God, please" by sending me someone who could immediately and honestly remind me what was important in life and point me back in the direction of God's peace. I smiled gratefully at Kim, and wiped my nose with the back of my hand.

"That'll teach you to buy the off-brand junk," she said.

Truer words were never spoken.

Ballet

Kim's pep talk was just the shot in the arm, the kick in the pants, that I needed. I was having a baby! God was blessing us with another amazing, unique, unrepeatable human being! This was reason to celebrate, not to sit around panicking.

I was amazed to discover that life pretty much went on normally despite the fact that, in my mind at least, our family was entering freak-show territory. Four children! By the time this newest one came, we'd have a six-year-old, a three-year-old, a one-year-old, and a newborn. I was like the Old Woman Who Lived in a Shoe.

Only, unlike her, I did know what to do. I was going to sign my daughter up for ballet, because it was a really good deal and lots of my friends' daughters were enrolled. I figured it would be a fun hour a week for Lotus, and the boys and I would enjoy spending time with friends in a church gym while class was under way.

It would be fun! It would be educational! It would be a pleasant social outing once a week. That's how it worked out in my head.

Confronted with the reality, I soon began to loathe ballet. I'd sit with the boys for an hour, trying to get them to stop picking things (normally bugs) off the floor and eating them. At first, I thought I'd distract them from bug-eating by bringing snacks. I soon stopped bringing snacks for them after almost killing a woman and her child with these same, seemingly innocent, snacks.

I knew this woman vaguely through the homeschool group—well enough to know that she and one of her children had a deadly allergy to peanuts. This fact sort of drifted through my mind on Thursdays, usually as we were headed to class (late), and the kids were eating an afternoon snack of—yes!—peanut butter sandwiches. Equal parts panicked and guilty, I'd vigorously scrub the children with baby wipes in the parking lot, praying that whatever danger was contained in the peanut oils would be neutralized by the chemicals in the wipes.

Then Lotus went into class, and the boys and I began our hour of time-wasting. In the beginning, I had thought to bring small snacks for the boys, plus enough to share with the other children there. The first time it was granola bars. I was congratulating myself for my stunning display of mommy-foresight when Allergy Woman looked at my snacks with horror as she was escorting her son away from the kill zone.

"Do those have *NUTS* in them???" she asked in an incredulous voice, as her son tried to avoid breathing. I stared blankly at her for a moment and then realized what I had done. I had armed seven children aged six and under with cashew-encrusted weapons. The woman and her son fled the room for the day, and I was left to ponder the depths of my insensitivity.

The next week, I was ready to make amends. I did not bring cashew-containing items. In fact, I went all the way in the opposite direction, and just brought plain old candy. Jelly Bellies, in fact. All went well until one of my six-and-under crowd pulled out a jellybean, chewed it for a moment, then happily called out, "Peanut Butter!"

Out went Allergy Woman and her son, throwing me, as I imagined, a dirty look.

For several weeks afterward, she didn't even bother coming into the waiting room. Snacks were consumed with glee, with no regard for safety, allergies, or nutritional value.

Then came the day of the parents' meeting. We were told by the ballet teacher that we would need to show up early for a brief talk about the upcoming recital. Since we were going to be there longer than usual, I packed several snacks, but was very, very careful not to bring them out until *after* the meeting, since I figured Allergy Woman would need to listen, too. The meeting ended, I took my boys out of ballet class, went several rooms over, waited a little bit longer, and then opened up snacks.

Not two minutes later, Allergy Woman walked into the room, *covering her nose and mouth with her hand and standing fifteen feet away from me,* saying that the ballet teacher had forgotten to have the moms sign off on something. She then placed the paper on the ground where she was and backed slowly away, as if she were afraid I was going to pelt her with peanut-butter-covered peanuts. For an ugly moment, I contemplated doing just that.

That's when I gave up. I stopped bringing snacks, and just let the boys eat bugs while I sat there, drearily convinced that God had planned several nasty allergies for baby number four, including one to peanuts.

Did I mention I hated ballet?

Poison Control

I'll spare you the suspense and disclose that baby number four did *not* have allergies. Thanks be to God, we've been spared that cross with all the kids so far, which is fantastic, since they have put everything into their mouths. Everything. In fact, despite the fact that I'm terrible at remembering strings of random numbers, I have the Poison Control hotline burned into my brain because I've called it so many times.

Growing up, I have only one memory of anyone calling Poison Control. My younger cousin had gotten into our pool-supply cabinet one summer day and was found with several chlorine tablets strewn about her general vicinity. All the adults feverishly tried to figure out if she'd eaten any of them. My mom called Poison Control, and I have no idea what happened, but my cousin was fine.

As I say, this was the only time this came up during my childhood, and I feel that "once" is a normal sort of number in this category.

I, on the other hand, am up to six calls in a mere decade as a parent. I feel that "six times" is a more alarming number.

The first time, we were visiting my in-laws' house. Lotus was three and was supposed to be napping in the master bedroom. Instead, she sauntered out with white, powdery residue all around her mouth. Ken and I got squinty-eyed and puzzled, wiping the stuff off her face with our fingers and trying to figure out what it was. It was my father-in-law who realized what had happened, as he went into the master bathroom and saw the mini-trail of destruction wrought by the not-sleeping toddler. He showed us a stick of deodorant, cap off, with several trenches dug into the stick—trenches that were the size of Lotus's finger.

Envisioning my tiny child succumbing to deodorant poisoning, I dialed Poison Control. As soon as a woman answered the phone, I found myself demonstrating a rambling, ditsy-sounding defensiveness.

"Hi. Um. My three-year-old just ate some deodorant? Secret. Like, the stick kind, not the wet roll-on stuff. In case that makes a difference? She was supposed to be napping, and we all thought she was napping, and there's four adults in the house right now—and none of us has been drinking—but somehow she snuck out of the bed and into the bathroom and got into the deodorant and I think ate it."

There was a pause, which I assumed was so the woman at the other end could trace my call and cue the police to head for my in-laws' house and prepare to arrest me for child endangerment.

"How much did she eat?" the lady finally asked. I've seen cop shows. I know she was just stalling long enough for the squad to get a fix on my location. And lucky for her, I babble when nervous.

"Um. Well, it's hard to say. There's a couple of gouges out of the stick."

"Did you see her eat any of it?"

"See her? No. She did it in the bathroom. But not like I usually let my three-year-old play in the bathroom. Just this once. But not on purpose. She—"

The woman cut me off. "Are you sure she even ate any?"

I wondered if maybe the full weight of this situation wasn't fully impressing itself upon my Poison Controller. "Well, it's smeared all over her face. And ... hang on a second. Lotus, come here, let me smell your breath. Yeah. I think her breath smells deodorant-y."

Did I hear the tiniest of sighs from the other end? Probably not. It was probably a signal to the SWAT team that had finally reached my in-laws' house and was now rappelling silently off the roof, preparing to smash through the windows and drag me, kicking and screaming, away from my deodorant-damaged child.

"Okay, so how much deodorant do you estimate she ate? Judging by what's missing from the stick. A tablespoon?"

"No," I said slowly, trying to imagine a tablespoon full of deodorant. By now, Lotus had wandered off to play with toys, seemingly unaffected by her impending nutritional doom.

I began to think I had overreacted, and I suddenly wanted to get off the phone.

"A teaspoon?" the woman suggested, sounding weary. I could see her, phone in one hand, massaging her forehead with the other. I took the out she gave me.

"No, looking at it, I think it was less than half a teaspoon. Probably nothing, really. In fact, she probably just smeared it on her face without eating any of it."

The voice at the other end perked up considerably. "I'm sure that's what it was," she said. "Really, a child wouldn't eat deodorant. It doesn't taste nice, and even if she ate some, the amount you described wouldn't harm her. If you notice any irritation around her mouth, flush the area with water."

"Sure. Sure thing," I said nonchalantly. And thus ended what I foolishly thought would be my last call to Poison Control. But since that time, the list of ingested items has grown with our family:

Windex (not a systemic poison);

RoundUp Home Defense Insect Spray (only possible side effect: irritated skin at point of contact, which the child in question didn't even suffer);

An Unmarked Pill, identified via the wonders of the Internet to be a generic cold medication (could possibly induce drowsiness, but given the child's age and weight, nothing more);

A Handful of Berries picked off the bayberry bush in the yard (keep child under observation in case of vomiting); and

Spackle (the oddest of all).

The spackle, which was left in a bathroom we were repainting because Ken foolishly insists on things like filling in nail-holes before repainting a room, was in a large bucket with a bright red lid.

I walked into the bathroom and discovered three-year-old Joaquin sitting on the bathroom floor, spackle bucket between his legs, with the red lid in one hand and a giant handful of spackle in the other. And a great smear of it on his face. He looked up at me and happily smiled, revealing teeth that were layered thick with spackle and a tongue that was grayish with it. I nearly went into labor right there.

I grabbed the child under one arm, picked up the phone with the other, and placed yet another call to Poison Control. There is a moment, between the placement of the call and the response on the other end, where thoughts race through your head. There's a brutal examination of your life. You ask yourself questions like, "How could I have birthed a child who found spackle palatable?" and, "What does this say about my cooking?" and "This is why I never bother to fill in nail holes prior to repainting a room."

In case you're wondering, spackle is not toxic and is in fact chemically similar to antacids such as *Tums* or *Rolaids*. So, while my child enjoyed a heartburn-free evening, I hid the spackle in the garage, in case he had developed a taste for it.

I slapped paint on the bathroom walls as quickly as I could, unfilled nail holes and all.

Jude

In between calls to Poison Control, ballet lessons during which I was seemingly poisoning others, and Friday playdates, the fourth pregnancy clicked right along until my due date … and right on past. Of course.

Why do doctors feel it necessary to provide specific due dates? Why not just a range of possibilities? Like, "Well, Mrs. Donaldson, given the date of your last period, and the fact that none of your children likes to vacate the premises, I'm going to say this child can be expected sometime between September 1 and November 2. I'm confident you won't go over."

That would be so much more psychologically bearable than one precise date.

Two days after the due date, I turned to Ken and insisted that immediately after Mass we were going to the zoo. Yes, it was early September in Memphis. Yes, it was still six million degrees outside. No, I didn't care. We were going to the dang zoo, and we weren't leaving until I was in labor.

Always one to pick his battles carefully, Ken didn't argue with the crazy woman, and so off went the five of us to the broiling-hot zoo. Where I didn't experience a single contraction during the entire afternoon.

We came home, fed the kids, put them to bed, and started watching something on the TV. Or rather, Ken watched. I pouted and glared at my abdomen.

Around 11 p.m. I told Ken I was going to bed. He said he was going to stay up and watch some more TV, since he didn't need to be at work until 3 p.m. the next afternoon. Sunday nights for us didn't have the same sense of bedtime urgency that they do for people with normal working hours.

I fell asleep, brooding about my uterus's refusal to act.

An unknown period of time later, I woke up in discomfort. A contraction strong enough to wake me was slowly making its way through my abdomen. In the dark, I made a face at it and scoffed. Please. It's going to take more than a measly contraction to get me worked up. I tried to go back to sleep, but another contraction stopped me.

Then another one.

And another one.

I judged the time between each to be between five to seven minutes. Ken wasn't in bed with me yet, so I figured that if I had five more contractions of the same intensity and frequency, I'd go get him to let him know we may have a situation on our hands.

Trial by Childbirth

Five contractions came and went. Just as my feet were about to touch the floor to go get him, Ken opened the door to the bedroom.

"Hey," I said softly in the dark. "What time is it?"

He told me it was shortly after one in the morning, and he was coming to bed. I told him he probably didn't want to do that, since I was in labor and we needed to get the show on the road.

He heaved a weary sigh, flipped on the lights, and started getting things ready.

I had arranged for Kim to come over and stay with the kids when I went into labor. When my due date came and went, she made sure her cell phone was constantly charged and on her, so she would be ready to hop in the car and head to my house. I felt the tiniest bit apologetic calling her now in the middle of the night, but judging by the contractions, she needed to get her sleepy butt over here and watch my kids so I could get to the hospital.

The phone rang. And rang. And rang. No one answered.

Weird.

I called my mom, who lived six hours away, and who had put me under strict orders to call as soon as I was in labor. She was out the door and in the car before I finished talking to her.

I called Kim again. Still nothing.

I tried her husband's cell phone. No answer.

The contractions were starting to get painful. And closer together. Ken grew increasingly agitated that we couldn't get hold of anyone to watch the kids. The hospital was a good thirty-five minutes away, even in the middle of the night, and there was no telling if I would last another hour before the new baby came.

I tried calling another friend.

No answer there, either.

Then, for an unknown reason, there descended over me the strangest cloud of calm I've ever felt. I told Ken that everything would be fine, but we had to get going. This meant waking three sleeping children aged six, three, and fifteen months, and taking them with us to the hospital.

I didn't know what would happen when we got there; maybe it would mean Ken sat with the kids in the waiting room while I labored and delivered by myself, but in the end, we'd have two things: a new baby and a great story to tell about it. Some distant part of me marveled at the change in me from my panic-filled first labor and this one, but there was no time for self-congratulation—this baby was coming.

Ken got the children into the van while I breathed through increasingly painful contractions. I could hear the kids, sleepy and confused and a little scared. Ken tried to keep them calm, murmuring, "The new baby's coming! Let's go to the hospital to meet the baby!" Lotus was the only one who bought into the excitement. Joaquin just snorted and fell back asleep, while Gabriel started to scream and throw his pacifier.

As I tried calling Kim again, Ken realized we had no gas in the van, so we'd have to stop for some before getting to the hospital.[13] As he pumped the gas, I realized that we were probably cutting things pretty close. I tried not to let my imagination run wild about Kim's failure to answer the phones. It *probably* wasn't a wild rhino, escaped from the zoo, rampaging through their house. Most likely it *wasn't* an outbreak of the Plague or

---

[13] Never assume that the parents of a large family will be "organized" or "prepared."

Trial by Childbirth

a zombie attack. But still ... two different phones ringing in the middle of the night? In a house of fourteen people, you'd think someone would have heard it.

Ken got back in the car. As he started driving, a new sort of pain spread down my back. The contractions went from painful to excruciating in a single moment. I tried to hide this development from him, because I could tell from the clench of his jaw that he was right there at the breaking point. I couldn't blame him. Sure, we were seasoned veterans at this child-birthing thing, but throwing three small children into the mix at 1 a.m. seemed a lot to ask.

We miraculously made it all the way to the hospital without having to pull off the highway to deliver the baby. Ken parked up front to let me out. I walked to the desk and started the check-in process while he parked and tried to get three small, terribly confused children out of the car and into the lobby.

I was brought to a room and asked the ridiculous series of questions they always pose at times like this. (Seriously? I need to tell someone once again when my last period was? How about this: Since I'm in the middle of some seriously painful contractions and all, why don't you just write down whatever date tickles your fancy and we can get this game underway?)

Fortunately, Ken was told that since the maternity wing was almost deserted, he could put the kids to bed in an empty room.

Ken tried to convince the savages that sleep was a stellar idea while I dealt with the nurse from *One Flew Over the Cuckoo's Nest*. She had me strapped up to a fetal monitor—she could clearly see that I was experiencing significant contractions. But STILL, she kept on with the questions.

"What are the birthdates and birth weights of your previous children?" was the one that pushed me over the edge.

"My previous children? You know what? You can go ask them. They're in the next room. With my husband, who's trying to get them to sleep. But before you go, I'd like a shot of Stadol, because I feel like my spine is being ripped out of my body. I'm not answering another question until I have my drugs and my husband."

She left, not hurrying to get my pain meds, while I tried to figure out why I was being such a giant wimp. This was my fourth time around—there was no good reason why I should be responding like this to contractions. It felt as if someone were dragging a rusty iron bar down my spine. My back was filled with radioactive lead. I was going to die right there, and the autopsy would reveal alien implants all along my backbone.

While I contemplated the mournful state of my alien-infested spine, the nurse returned—with Ken! I don't think I was ever so happy to see him in my whole life.

Nurse Excellent Bedside Manner gave me my drugs and asked Ken the rest of her "Top 1,000 Most Useless Questions." While he answered her, I dissolved into pain that was never ever going to end.

Finally, I croaked at him, "Have her check me. I think I need an epidural."

Never. Never in the history of my labors had I said those words. I think Ken almost fainted.

The nurse checked me, and I was at lucky number seven. That's the place where you're so close to being done that by the time you're prepped for the epidural, things may be over anyway.

I rolled over in misery. I waved my hand irritably at follow-up questions about the epidural.

Then, just like that, it was time to push.

The nurse checked me and called for the doctor.[14] Then all the frantic motions that I associate with the pushing stage began.

Ken and Doctor Black had decided that Ken could take an active role in delivering this baby. I guess by the time your fourth rolls around, cutting the cord doesn't do it. You want to be right there, getting your hands dirty. And your arms, and your elbows, your shoulders ... So Ken and the good doctor stationed themselves at the ready, and I pushed. Only this time, this first time in my whole life, pushing hurt.

A lot.

By the time you push, the pain is supposed to go away. What the hell was wrong?

I pushed again.

This time, my bag of waters, which was still intact, exploded all over the room like something horrible from a Gallagher shtick. I would have died of embarrassment, but I know for a fact that some of it got on Nurse Asks a Million Questions, so I was sort of happy.

As a result of the eruption of Mt. Amniotic Fluid, my cervix collapsed back down to eight centimeters. So we had to wait a few contractions for it to dilate fully again. During this time, when I was in extreme, unexpected pain, Nurse Not Going to Win Miss Congeniality, who had toweled herself off and gotten far away from any part of me that would possibly hose her down again, stationed herself next to my left ear, leaning on the monitor.

And then she began drumming her fingernails on the plastic.

[14] Sweet Doctor Black, who had only just sauntered into the hospital.

No, seriously. I want you to contemplate my words. This gesture, interpreted by every single human being on the planet as an indication of impatience, was being made by a "professional," because she had to suffer the indignity of waiting a couple of minutes for the show to get back on the road.

And then, another nurse started snapping her gum!

Anyone who has tried to concentrate her way through profound pain understands how important silence is. Sure, in some cases, like a soldier in the middle of a battlefield, let's say, you can't count on it, but for the love of sweet Baby Jesus, couldn't the nursing staff hold off with the finger-drumming and the gum-smacking for the space of two contractions?!?!...

Whew. I'm over it now, really.

Anyway, eventually it was time to push again, and the pain was still there. I started to panic. Real, down-to-my-bones panic. I asked Ken what was wrong. He assured me that everything was fine. I knew he was a liar.

Then I heard Doctor Black casually (*casually!*) remark to Ken, "If this were a first-time mom, we'd be scheduling the emergency C-section now." Then the two of them were up to their shoulders in me, and suddenly, the baby's head was out.

Facing us all.

The baby was posterior! Knowing that the pain I'd been feeling was nothing more exotic than a baby skull scraping its way down my spine, I rallied, pushed again, and Jude was born.

There was Ken, holding the baby he had delivered. He laid the baby on my chest, and I started that indecipherable litany of thanksgiving all new mothers recite as I held my little son for the first time.

Someone opened the door to the room, and there was a wide-eyed Lotus, standing outside. She came in and met her new baby brother while I called my mom (who had covered half the six-hour drive already) to tell her that her new grandson had been born.

Things settled down, the room cleared out, and the baby and I got some rest. A few hours later, I tried calling Kim again, and this time got an answer.

"Hey!" I said. She said hey back, clearly wondering why I was calling so early.

"Jude Thomas was born a few hours ago!" I told her.

She told me I was a filthy liar.

"No, seriously! He's here, and he's beautiful."

She asked why we didn't call her. I told her I'd tried, but no one ever answered. She spent a few moments cursing the phone company, then told me how sorry she felt.

"Don't be sorry. It was fine. Everything worked out perfectly, and now I've got this amazing story to tell!"

A great story wasn't enough for Kim, who made me promise that I'd let her host the baptism party. I may be many things, but I'm no dummy. I told her we had a deal, hung up the phone, and buried my nose on the top of Jude's head, which, like all newborn babies' heads, smelled of eternity.

8

∞

After the Tipping Point, It's All a Blur

While I try and try, I cannot remember the reasons I had for not wanting children. I can't remember what I was scared of, or what I thought I would give up by opening my life to *life*. Certainly, it was chaotic. Absolutely, it was intense. There were times that I thought I'd run screeching out the front door and disappear into the night. If I hadn't been so utterly exhausted. But there was so much beauty in that time, too. So much laughter and wonderment, more than enough to carry us over the rough patches.

There was the realization that Joaquin was praying to Our Lady of Breakfast, which I arrived at one day when I really listened to him saying the Hail Mary. His version went like this:

Hail Mary, full of grace, the Lord is with thee!
Breakfast art thou among women,
And breakfast is the fruit of your womb, Jesus! . . .

It makes perfect sense, in its way.

There was the phase Lotus went through, when, for some reason, she wore an eye patch nonstop and also refused to listen to any book other than A *Midsummer Night's Dream*. I'd catch her out in the backyard, standing in the sandbox in 90-degree weather and 200 percent humidity, eye patch over her left eye, declaring to an imaginary Puck that he needed to go find the juice of a particular purple flower.

There were moments when I'd laugh so hard I'd cry. Like the morning Joaquin came sauntering into the bedroom in green, stripey, footie pajamas (with holes in both feet), a gun holster around his tiny, four-year-old waist (with the holsters on backward, so the gun handles were knocking into each other in front of him), a wooden sword jammed into the back of his pajamas, hilt protruding eight inches over his right shoulder, a red light saber in one hand, and a paint stick in the other.

"Good morning, lady. I am Prince Phillip," he said.

I was momentarily dizzy from the number of toy weapons the boy had accumulated. "Good morning, Prince Phillip." I managed to keep my voice steady, but I could feel my stomach quivering in mirth.

"I am here to protect your kingdom," Prince Phillip solemnly announced.

"Really? That's great." As I was unable to immediately think of any threat the kingdom currently faced, we stared blankly at one another for a moment. "Prince Phillip, I love you. Do you have a wife?" He nodded yes.

"She's back at my castle. She's the queen. Princes have to marry queens."

"Oh," I said. "Makes sense. Do you have any children?" Again Prince Phillip nodded. "Oh. What are their names?"

"There's Junior, Wookie—" I cut him off.

"Excuse me, did you say Wookie?" He nodded. "Oh. Junior and Wookie. Those are nice names—"

He held up a hand to stop me. "There are more. There's Ellie and Terrie and Pah'ee."

"Ellie and Terrie and Pah'ee?" There was a little tremor in my voice. (That's "Pah'ee" as in "Potty.")

Thankfully, he didn't seem to notice. "Yes. Them. Would you like to meet them? I have a long horse that can fit them all so they can come meet you."

He wandered out of the room. From the living room, I heard him call to his five children to get on the horse. They must have been spectacularly well-behaved children, because he returned in no time, introducing me to Junior, Wookie, Ellie, Terrie, and Pah'ee.

Ken, who had now woken up, asked the prince what the horse's name was.

"He doesn't have one," the prince responded.

"A horse with no name, huh?" said I. "Someone should make a song about that." I thought this was funny; the prince was not amused.

"Well. Her name is … Darren." He looked up at me quickly. "Is Darren a girl's name?"

I shrugged uncertainly. "I guess so."

A sliding noise was then heard coming down the hall. Gabriel appeared in the doorway, dragging an object that the boys had alarmingly dubbed their "weapons box" (an empty case of diapers from Costco). Gabriel was apparently the dutiful, dim-witted sidekick.

Prince Phillip instructed his page to take the weapons box back to the castle, but not before I heard the unmistakable sound of jingle bells coming from the box.

"What's jingling in there? Do you have a weapon that *jingles*?"

Prince Phillip nodded. "Yes. That's what the animals use to signal to me that there is an evil giraffe I have to slay."

"Evil giraffe?"

"Yes." He said very seriously. "It happens all the time."

There was a day eighteen-month-old Gabriel was feeling particularly "out of sorts." That's what I called days when he reverted to his awesome babyhood and screamed all day long.

I gave him a bath that night, which seemed to put him in good spirits. Until the bath was over, when he resumed screaming something at the top of his lungs. I didn't need a translator to tell me it was toddler swear-words.

Once I got him into his pajamas, which was done only by pinning him down in a wrestling move I used to see on WWF, I set him loose on the house. I watched him run from my room, kicking and punching anything in his way.

Suddenly I remembered that Jude—sweet, defenseless baby Jude—was lying on the floor in the living room. I rushed after Gabriel, sure that I knew where this was heading, but too far behind to prevent it. Gabriel tore over to his brother, just as I was preparing to vault over the couch to block Jude from the kick I was sure was coming.

Still screaming and crying, Gabriel threw himself on the floor next to his baby brother and put his head next to Jude's. He then gave Jude a big, yet gentle(-ish) hug, and his screaming and baby-swearing stopped. He gave his brother a big, slobbery kiss on the mouth, and I saw his toddler body relax. The two brothers lay there quietly together on the floor, calm and happy in each other's company.

Truly, the best gift you can give your child is a sibling.

Eventually, Ken and I realized that the house we had bought for a tidy family of four was bursting at the seams. The dining room had been pressed into service as a classroom, which, since the breakfast nook in the kitchen couldn't hold all six of us, meant that meals were eaten among science projects and artwork. The bedrooms were on a constant rotation as we tried to figure out the best sleeping arrangements. The acoustics of the house were such that if someone spoke downstairs, everyone upstairs could hear it. What was "charmingly cramped" was rapidly turning into something less endearing.

Looking back, we could have done some weekend-warrior projects to turn the office/TV room into an acceptable sleeping space, thus upping us to a four-bedroom house, but it was more fun to consider moving. Ken and I had aspirations to get a couple of acres, start some gardens, raise some chickens, and sort of create a farmhouse to go along with our zoo.

We made an offer on a rambling five-bedroom at the end of a dirt road, near a bunch of trailers. But the real-estate bubble had just burst, and we had to let our option on it expire—we couldn't sell our own house. So we stayed and decided to be thankful for our blessings. It was a good house, and we would make it work.

Our resolve lasted about half a year. Then the restlessness set in again, and we thought we'd start innocently looking at the real-estate market again. Just looking. Like window-shopping. Only instead of looking from the outside, we made arrangements with a real-estate agent to look from the inside.

Looking at houses from the inside is always a mistake. If we'd just kept our noses out of the houses we'd never had found The House. But we didn't, and we did, and once we saw The House we couldn't un-see it.

The House was in a nice neighborhood, with zero condemned mobile homes to be found. The layout of the house was sensible and custom-made for a large family. There was room for school, room to spread out, room to do everything our house-crazy hearts could desire.

We made an offer, which was accepted, and we tried to scheme a way to sell our house in the most dismal market in ten billion years. I'd sit with my sister-in-law over dinner and dream about the new house with her.

"We could just foreclose on this house," I said, while she raised her eyebrows at me over her ice tea. "It's not the big stigma that it used to be. Not now. Not with everything going on." She shook her head at me. I sighed. What had we been thinking, making an offer on a house before ours had sold?

"If it's meant to be, the house will sell," she said, and I sighed again. A month on the market, and we hadn't had a single viewing. And our homeowner association prohibited renting our house to help cover the mortgage, so that possibility was gone.

"I don't know what we were thinking, Debra," I said dramatically. She just raised her eyebrows again and shrugged.

The phone rang, and I was grateful for the change of subject. I didn't want to dwell on the stupidity of the financial timebomb we'd crafted for ourselves.

It was Ken.

"Drugs," I said, which was met with silence from his end.

"Drugs?" he eventually asked.

"Drugs!" I said, warming up to my subject. "One of us is going to have to sell drugs to pay for the second mortgage. And it'll probably be you, because you're the one who leaves the house regularly. I'm surrounded by kids all day, and I draw the line at selling drugs to children."

"I think everyone here at work who's got a habit already has a dealer," Ken observed.

"We could have competitive pricing. Maybe offer coupons?"

"Hey, forget about the drugs for a second. Are you sitting down?"

"Sitting down? No, I'm standing in the kitchen, looking at your sister, who is making faces at me about my drug-dealing idea. You'd think she was a former cop or something."[15]

"Well, maybe you should sit down." I didn't like where this conversation was going. I grew surly, to hide my fear.

"I'm not going to sit down. I may be done with sitting for the rest of my life. Now what do you have to tell me?"

What he had to tell me was that we were being transferred. He had just been called into his boss's office and told that a transfer was in the works.

I stood there, resting my head against the window. "When?" I asked.

"I don't know. Could be three months, could be three weeks. I'll know by Friday."

"Well, that's wonderful news." I mumbled. "What are we going to do about the house contract?"

"I don't know. Probably just have to break the contract and lose our earnest money, I guess." I swore softly under my breath.

"Okay. Well, your sister's here, and she's probably wondering why I'm banging my head against the window right now, so . . ." We said our goodbyes and hung up.

I turned around to look at Debra.

"So," she said, "a transfer, huh?"

Cops, man. There's no use in hiding things from them.

Before I could answer, the phone rang again. It was my real-estate agent, who had just gotten some paperwork on the history of the house we were buying.

"Flooded," she said. "A portion of the house flooded at one time. And it wasn't on his disclosure statement."

---

[15] She is.

I rubbed the bridge of my nose with one hand, and made a "Bring me more beer! Stat!" motion at my sister-in-law with the other.

"So what does that mean?" I asked.

"Well, it means a couple things. One, it means the property now may need to carry flood insurance, which is never cheap." Here, I just dropped my head onto the table, too dejected even to take the beer Debra had brought me.

"It also means that if you'd like to break the contract, you could, and not forfeit your earnest money, because the man failed to mention the flooding in the disclosure statement."

I jerked my head up off the table.

"We could ... *break the contract?*" My heart was fluttering in my chest. The agent affirmed that possibility. I calmly told her I'd talk it over with Ken and get back to her tomorrow, then hung up the phone.

There was absolute silence in the house for a moment. Then I burst into jubilant whooping, causing all the kids to come running to see what was going on.

God had provided us a way to untangle ourselves from the stupid, possibly dire financial sinkhole we had gotten ourselves into! God was awesome!

Then, Ken's call came back to mind, and I put my head back down on the table. A transfer. We were leaving Mississippi. We were leaving. That was significantly less awesome.

On Being Open to Life

Not long after this, my parents came to visit. My dad and I were talking about the transfer, about how I was taking it, about how the kids were taking it. He got sort of serious and asked me, "So how many more kids do you and Ken think you'll have?"

After the Tipping Point, It's All a Blur

It was a totally fair question, coming from a man whose daughter had been married with the intention of never having children. A daughter who had then caught religion and had gone and converted to *Catholicism* of all things. A daughter who now had four children in the space of six years.

I did not consider his question very carefully, I'm sad to say. I sort of shrugged and gave a flippant reply about "how long until menopause?" and we drifted to other topics. It was all I could do to wrap my mind around moving—the thought of setting a final number on my offspring was too much for me to handle.

In bed that night, I thought about the question some more. How many more kids *did* Ken and I think we'd have? The answer that I kept coming back to, no matter which way I approached the question was, "*I don't know.*"

I didn't know how many more children I'd have. I couldn't even tell you how many more children I *wanted* to have. And then I realized with a shock that I was okay with that.

When I converted and started fumbling my slow and painful way through the Church's teachings on human sexuality, I labored under the same assumptions many people have—the Church says sex is only to be for procreation, not recreation; the Church says you have to have as many babies as you can; the Church keeps women in a medieval state of perpetual pregnancy because it is a misogynistic organization.

It was only the grace of God that helped me toward baptism, dragging that load of baggage with me. Without supernatural help, I would have hightailed it out of Catholic-land faster than you can say, "Buy stock in Huggies!"

But the more I learned about the holistic view the Church has of sex—how she embraces and celebrates both the biological and emotional aspects of it, the more fascinated I became.

I first stumbled across pornography as a seven-year-old, and the images in that magazine were burned into my heart in horrified shame. I grew up surrounded by a culture that pushed the Pill and said abortion was a woman's "choice" and that filming people having sex and consuming it as entertainment was a "healthy expression of sexuality."

Yet at the same time, I was told that it was important to have sex with "someone you love," that fidelity was important, and that divorce was something to be strongly avoided.

Growing up with such a schizophrenic view of sex is not only confusing—it is exhausting. We are designed to be rational creatures capable of logical thought. To convince myself that sex was special enough to save for someone I loved, and to keep that activity confined to that relationship, while at the same time being comfortable with people selling images of sex as a commodity—and perhaps selling them to my beloved sex partner—made my head quietly explode. Welcome to secular sex.

So when I learned that the Church did not only *not* hate sex, but that she actually taught that it was an amazing, earthmoving thing, I didn't believe it. I mean, come on! What about all those jokes in movies? Many a truth is spoken in jest and all that, right? And the archetype of the repressed nun? Or the Catholic schoolgirl, gone wild as a righteous revolt against the sexually stifling religious culture? Surely this cultural shorthand couldn't be wrong. (Could it?)

I did what all rational people should do—I educated myself. I had gotten an education about sex from the culture; now I'd let Catholicism show me what it had.

What it had was amazing. It had understanding about the dignity given to each person, and the gift God gave us in sex, and how it was designed—deliberately and divinely designed— both to create new life and to deepen the bonds between husband and wife. It was something profound, sublime, and untamable, as all things in direct contact with God are. Seeing sex from that point of view makes a person reckless—by the culture's standards, anyway. Seeing sex as a powerful, consuming gift from God makes you do that rashest of things—allowing yourself to be open to life. It's such a cliché, at least in the circles I ran in then, and yet it took me a while to understand it.

Being open to life means a married couple's being generous in welcoming children into their lives. It means trusting that God will give you strength to walk with Him when you're blessed with a girl, then a boy, and then you hear people wonder aloud why you're still having more. It means trusting that God has a plan for each of His children when you realize that you're not going to be able to pay for college tuitions. It means trusting that God keeps us, as Psalm 17 says, as close as the pupil of His eye, even on days when you've run out of diapers and four kids are fighting like cats and dogs and you need to go grocery shopping but all you want to do is run away to some imaginary glittery life in Provence or Moscow or somewhere.

(Glittery? Moscow? I did say we're talking imaginary here.)

That is what being open to life means. It means being open to life, *all of it*, from the babies to the toddlers to the tweens to the spouses. Being open to them—that is, striving to love them as God loves them. When a new baby is born around here, being open to life involves all these thoughts:

1. Look at the baby! The baby is perfect and amazing, and I cannot believe how blessed we are to have been given him!

2. Look at the baby! The baby is perfect and amazing, and I really love how his brothers and sister adore him. I cannot believe how blessed we are to have been given this family!

3. Look at the baby! He eats a lot. I don't really remember what sleep was like. The house is a total mess, and if I don't get some sort of order imposed on my household, I'm pretty sure I'm going to lose it. But, still, we're blessed and all that … but I think I have enough blessings now.

4. I would kill someone for four hours of sleep in a row. And I still really need to get some sort of order imposed on this household. Blah, blah, blah, blessings. I'm done with this childbearing business.

5. ORDER OR DEATH! Everyone has a written schedule, work routines are followed with strict discipline, meals are absolutely nutritious but uninspired—who needs blessings? I've got an iron fist with which to rule this house!

6. Order is cool, but so is spontaneity. A nice little routine has again fallen over the house, and I'm finding myself managing to remember gratitude. Life is sweet, isn't it?

7. Look at the baby! He's not a baby anymore! He's walking! He's sleeping through the night! The house has completely and utterly absorbed him into its routine!

8. I do head counts of children and always come up one short. I have to be reminded it's because we only have X number children, and I'm counting one higher.

9. I realize the family is so beautiful and so amazing that I want another child to know this love.

That's how it always goes. The amount of time it takes me to get from point 1 to point 9 varies, but over four children, the road had been the same.

So, lying there in bed that night, trying to figure out the answer to my dad's question, I was surprised to find myself not fearing the possibility of having more children. I realized that God waited so patiently for me to adjust and grow, and He never once pushed me into anything. I realize that for a while after the last birth, I was only "open to life" in the most nebulous, abstract sort of ways, and that was okay with God—He would wait.

We were leaving our home. To where, no one knew yet, or at least the people who knew weren't telling. But there was chaos looming on the horizon; that much was certain. There was chaos in the form of packing and loading and goodbying and house hunting and all sorts of unpleasantness. It was coming, and I was shocked to realize I was open to it, because it was life, and it was ultimately under God's control. It was a good life, and I was deeply grateful for it.

I didn't need to know how many children I would be given. I didn't even need to know how many I wanted. Why would I need that information, when instead I had the absolute assurance that God was with me, and with my marriage, and that He keeps us as close as the pupil of His eye?

On a Road to Nowhere

Kansas City. Missouri or Kansas side—we got to pick. Not that it mattered, because I didn't want to move, but giant, multinational corporations don't ask for my opinion on transfer decisions, shockingly.

The whole thing made me sick to my stomach. As much as I tried to remind myself that this was part of God's plan and ultimately would be used for good, it still made me sick. The thought of moving, the thought of finding a new house, in a new city, and having to leave behind all the amazing people God had brought into my life made me constantly feel that I was one bad smell away from throwing up.

Stress and nausea. Tears and nausea. Panic and nausea. Finally suspicious (and nauseated), I took a pregnancy test. Which was, predictably, positive.

So now, because it would have been so boring to deal with just a transfer, we got to deal with a pregnancy and a transfer. I did what I could. I eyeballed God from my seat on the couch and muttered about being open to life. I learned about home-schooling laws in Missouri vs. Kansas, to see which state was friendlier. I found a fantastic, hundred-year-old mansion, right across the street from a beautiful old parish. The house was being foreclosed on and could be had for a song, and I added it to the short list of properties I wanted to see once the time came. I made contact with homeschooling groups and got recommendations for doctors and parks and grocery stores and such.

I found myself astounded to discover that I was almost excited about moving. The chance to move into a more suitable house! An orthodox, Catholic homeschool group already contacted! Several pro-life doctors to interview and choose from! It was, as far as unexpected transfers go, not a bad deal.

And then we waited. Things got very weird at Ken's work, and suddenly, what was originally presented as a sure thing, in the works, and no turning back, morphed into something less certain. Ken and I were both on edge. He wanted to leave Memphis. I didn't know what I wanted. As my uncertainty grew, I defaulted to a desire to stay. Ken and I started bombarding God with dueling prayers at every Mass. I would glare at my husband out of the corner of my eye when we knelt on the kneelers, and hiss at him, "Stop praying for that. I'm going to out-pray you anyway. Concentrate on an intention you can win. Like the lottery or something."

He'd pretend he couldn't hear me.

Then, a month after placing that phone call telling me we were moving, Ken was told that we weren't. The position was filled by another employee, which meant Ken, and the rest of the Donaldson family, got to stay right where we currently were.

Reactions were mixed. Lotus was giddy and relieved. I was giddy and confused. Joaquin and Gabriel were confused. Jude was preverbal and couldn't care less where he lived, as long as there was access to food. Ken, however, was disappointed. And angry. And suddenly hell-bent on getting transferred somewhere, anywhere, as long as it was out of Memphis.

I was sad that he was so upset and unhappy with his work environment, but at the same time I was too happy to be staying to feel guilty. I looked around at everything God had done with our lives here in Memphis, and realized I couldn't imagine leaving. *There* was the parish where we entered the Church and baptized our babies. *There* was the pizza place where I had my pre-conversion tear-fest over the death of Pope John Paul II. *There*, ten miles down the road, lived our best friends. How could I want to leave a place that was the backdrop for epic changes in my marriage, my soul, and my world?

Ken would nod politely when I told him all this, then tell me he had applied for another transfer. One to Indiana, another to North Carolina. Neither position panned out, and I just stopped worrying about it, too busy putting down deeper roots to honestly contemplate moving. I did what Jesus said to do—let tomorrow worry about tomorrow.

And then, one tomorrow like every other, the call came. This time, it came while Ken was home, so he got to field it. He uttered a few terse words, hung up the phone, then turned to me, dazed.

"We're being transferred to Connecticut," he said.

With that, my world fell down around me.

Part 3

∞

Connecticut

9

∾

Mission Territory

Ken left Memphis forever, with a handful of houses printed off the Internet that we thought looked interesting. I liked a house that had been built in 1650. Ken did not. He swore that something that old had no choice but to be haunted, and he wasn't setting foot in a haunted house.

The kids and I dropped him off at the airport, and they sobbed as I pulled away. I had no idea how long it would be until they saw their daddy again. Depending on how the house search went, it could be a few weeks, or it could be months. And even the possibility of a short separation was bittersweet, since it meant leaving our home and our friends, a fact that was hitting Lotus particularly hard.

I went home by way of the library, hoping to boost our morale with books, but not even that helped. We were a sad group, four small children and one heavily pregnant mother, dejectedly flinging ourselves onto the couch to stare at pages of stories we weren't really reading.

A few days later, Ken called with news about the house search.

"I'm scheduled to go look at your haunted house tomorrow," he said, "but I don't think I'll need to. I think I found our house." He described it to me, sent me some pictures over e-mail, and I looked at them numbly. The whole thing seemed like something I was observing it from space—far away and affecting me only in the most theoretical manner.

I wore that feeling of detachment like a cloak for my final weeks in Mississippi. When construction crews came to replace the roof and install new windows, I observed with profound detachment. When the man from the moving company came to inventory the house and schedule the crew, I was distant. When my dad showed up to help me on the multiday road trip from Memphis to Hartford, I was barely there. None of it seemed real.

Even when I stood on Kim's driveway and hugged all of them goodbye, I couldn't shake the fog. I could feel tears on my face, I could tell my heart hurt, but none of it made sense. There was no way for me to wrap my mind around the fact that we were leaving. Leaving Memphis—the place God chose as the backdrop for our conversion, the place that saw our family grow from four to seven, the place that housed a golden bubble of devout Catholics that I knew was unique in space and time.

I got into the car, made sure all the kids were buckled up, and left Memphis for the last time, with Kim's face glowing in the light of my taillights.

Signs of Life

To say that the next few months were difficult would be an absurd understatement. We spent the first two weeks in an Extend-A-Stay while we waited to close on the house. Four children, one seven-months-pregnant woman, a man, and an extremely hyperactive Labrador puppy all set up a refugee-style existence in adjoining rooms. The view from our windows was an abandoned factory, now covered in swastikas and spray-painted with racial epithets. The flu tore through at one point, rendering five of us moaning masses of bodily fluids and forcing me to brave the lobby Laundromat at two in the morning the moment I felt well enough to wobble down the elevator.

Our mini-stay in Purgatory eventually came to an end, and we were able to move into our house. Our beautiful house, set in a beautiful valley, in what is hands-down the most beautiful place we've ever lived. Rivers and oceans and mountains surround us. Hiking trails and museums galore waited to be visited, once the new baby came.

But it was that unborn baby and the other four already walking around who brought into sharp focus a strange hostility that bubbled under the surface of life in our new state.

Back in Memphis, we existed in an amazing, unique social bubble. God had led our family into contact with people who embraced life, who participated fully with it, and who understood in a firsthand way the blessings that came with children. Back in Memphis, when I ran into people who didn't have large families, the reaction was generally one of wistfulness, wishing that they had had more themselves. The large, sprawling, sometimes beautiful mess of a big family was taken in typical low-key, Southern fashion.

In Connecticut, however, when our family came into view, we got outright stares, muttered-but-audible comments ("Good lord"; "Oh my God, how many *are* there?"). Complete strangers stopped us in the middle of our daily lives to demand to know the ages of the children, how I "did it," and then informed me that they disapproved of my family size. All of this, of course, was expressed in front of my children. I can't count how many adults the kids saw looking at them with intense expressions of disgust — as if their very existence was something offensive.

I'm not a thin-skinned woman. I don't need bland approval from strangers. But what we experienced in that first year in New England was not your typical thoughtless, "Hey, don't you know what causes that?" Or "Don't you have a TV?" It wasn't even your slightly more antagonistic, "So are you done yet?" or "Is he going to get fixed after this one?" It was something much more intense, much more aggressive.

Our neighborhood put on a group Easter egg hunt a few weeks after we moved in, where I met one of my new neighbors. The course of happy chatting revealed that both of us had sons who refused to wear any other footwear than cowboy boots. For a few moments, we cheerfully found refuge in each other, since five-year-old boys who will not wear anything but cowboy boots are sometimes a challenge. But then, as my kids came up to me one at a time, I noticed the woman's body language changing.

"How many do you have?" the lady said, scanning the herd of kids, trying to do the mental math and tote up all the kids who had come up to me during our conversation.

"Four," I said, "and this one's due in three weeks." I said, motioning toward the giant swell of baby under my shirt. She stared at me for a split second.

"You're insane," she said flatly. I waited a moment, to see if her words were going to be paired with a smile, or another comment, or *anything* to help us move past this social roadblock. Nothing came.

What do you do at that point? What do you do when a complete stranger announces that you are crazy and then expects you to continue on as if you agree? There was no follow-up for me to put the comment in context. No moral framework for her judgment, no "overpopulation" theories, no explanation or excuse.

Mission Territory

At Lowe's, we passed a car with a bumper sticker that read, "Cats, NOT Kids." The ceiling in one of the examination rooms at my OB/GYN had another bumper sticker affixed to it, proclaiming, "Condoms are easier to change than diapers." I wondered where the sister sticker was, which would read, "Broken diapers don't result in unplanned pregnancies."

The kids and I went to Whole Foods one day. They were super-excited, since a trip to Whole Foods always ended with their picking out something from the bakery. And so, shopping over, we left, all of them anticipating eating the little pastries safely stored in a plastic box cradled in Joaquin's hands.

We passed an old man on our way out. He was walking in, with reusable bags tucked under his arm, a hearing aid in one ear, and stooped-over posture telling of back trouble.

He stopped us as we passed by—loudly counting the kids, pointing at each one as he did so. This happened a lot in our new home. So much so that two-year-old Jude thought it was a real-life version of Sesame Street or Dora.

Still counting, the man got to my obvious bump that told the world, "It's a baby, she's not just in need of some exercise."

"*Five?!*" he demanded in a harsh voice.

I smiled at him. "Yes sir," I said. I didn't trust myself to say more.

At my response, he literally threw his hands up to the skies and made a retching noise. *A retching noise.* Then he stomped off.

And my children, bless them, didn't even react. Either their focus was so firmly on the pastries that they didn't notice, or they had become accustomed to adults reacting with physical disgust at their existence. The thought made me want to sink down to the ground right there and start crying.

I tried to puzzle out what exactly it was they were angry with. When I had one or two children, I never had such encounters. Was there, perhaps, something dangerous and awful about my other kids that I didn't see? After having a girl and a boy, was it possible that any other kids I may have simply were redundant? I had enough people tell me that once they got their child of the "missing" sex, they were done. Was there something to that? That sex trumped the individual worth of each person? Were Gabriel and Jude pointless because I already had Joaquin?

So that's where I was when our first New England Easter came to find me. I was at a place where I was angrier at myself for being so affected by the reactions of strangers than I was at the strangers. After all, Ken and I did not plan our family for the approval of others. We believed God when He told us that children are a blessing. We knew that our fifth child was just as meaningful and wondrous as our first. A life is not more or less important because of birth order.

But all these are just words. They're just slogans I say to try to rally morale, and they were hollow and bitter as I repeated them while getting ready for Mass on Easter Sunday. Particularly not helpful was the fact that Jude was a raging beast that morning. He was having allergic reactions to something in his new environment, and his eyes and nose were leaking some fluid usually seen only in horror movies.

We got to Mass, and I tried very hard not to assume that we were the largest family in the parish, that we stuck out like some traveling circus of oddities. Maybe some of the families had taken the smart road and split up for Mass — Mom took some to the early one, Dad took the rest to the later one. Certainly this is what we should have done — or so I think to myself as

Jude begins screaming to be let "DOWN!" before the opening prayer is even said.

Since it was Easter, the church was fuller than usual, and so the pew we thought we had to ourselves was soon shared with an older couple to our left, and then an older couple to our right. This guaranteed that the seven hundred bathroom trips we would have to take with Gabriel would be more disruptive.

Somehow, despite all that, despite Jude's slobbery nose and irritable mumbling, despite Gabriel's frequent demands to go to the bathroom, I was able to hear part of Father's homily. He spoke about the far-reaching ramifications of Easter, saying, "When I die and stand before God, He's not going to haul out some giant book and go over every single mistake I ever made. What He will do is look at me, and say, 'Michael, what did you do for me? What did you do to manifest my love to the world?'"

And this was the part where I started to cry a little. That was the part where I realized that when it's my turn to stand in front of God, and He asks me that question, I can say to Him, "I was open to the lives you wanted to bring into the world through me. I rose above my self-centered nature just enough to let You bring the blessings of these children into my life. I was sometimes scared and sometimes angry, and always at a loss about how I was going to mother these children, but I had hope that it would be Your grace, and not my shortcomings, that would triumph."

I managed to get myself under control in time for Communion. Jude was still screaming; Ken and I had been awesome tag-team partners in the liturgical rodeo. As I walked up to receive our Lord in the Eucharist, Joaquin's hand in my left, Gabriel's hand in my right, I felt a tap on my shoulder. I turned around and saw a silver-haired lady smiling at me.

"I had five children," she whispered to me. "I know where you are right now. Five children, and I never regretted it."

I looked at her, crying again, and told her, "Thank you" from the bottom of my heart. "I'm always so grateful to have mothers of large families telling me that they made it through," I whispered back at her. She smiled again and patted me on the shoulder. I was still crying a little as I received the Host, and I thought that if we routinely saw grace working in our souls, we would probably die of joy.

I didn't return to the pew, but instead took Joaquin and Jude into the "quiet room" for the remainder of Mass. They were, in fact, quiet as they happily played with the toys there. As I went to sit down, another woman, one who had either been in the pew with us, or directly behind, walked up to me.

"I had six," she says, smiling at the boys. "Six in eight years. Your children are all beautiful, and they were so well behaved." I stared at her for a moment and could only point an accusing finger at Jude. She smiled again. "He was fine. Poor little thing has allergies; what can you do?" She, too, patted me on the shoulder and walked off, leaving me a sobbing mess again.

Mass ended, and Ken, Lotus, and Gabriel came into the quiet room. As the four kids picked up the toys, Ken told me that another woman who had been sitting by us pulled him aside and gave him a similar pep talk. Mother of five, our children were beautiful, we were doing a great job. He told her that Jude had picked that precise Mass to display the worst behavior we had ever seen. She shook her head and repeated, "They're all beautiful."

As we left the church, I remembered something I had read a few days before, which referred to Christ's Cross as the "throne" from which He would rule the world. I hated those words then, particularly in light of the fact that we're all given crosses to carry, and those who refuse to carry them are not worthy to be called a disciple. Who wants a cross to be his throne? Good grief, ask me to carry it, I guess, but don't ask me to turn it into something glorious.

But on Easter, as I looked at my big, beautiful family and realized once again that it set me apart in this place, I suddenly understood what a throne does. It allows you to sit up a bit higher to give you a longer perspective than you would have without it. And that perspective, coupled with God's inexhaustible grace, is designed to help you find your way Home.

For now, God was asking us to call Connecticut home. He had led us to Mississippi, where a lifetime of seeds burst into bloom in the hothouse protection of our little Catholic bubble. Now He had led us out of that small Eden, to come be a witness to a life led by Christ. If we were a traveling carnival freak-show by New England standards, then we were going to be a carnival freak-show for Jesus.

I was ready. But first we needed to get Jude some allergy medicine, because his runny nose and gooby eyes were taking things to a whole level of freak-show that not even I was ready to deal with.

John-Luke

We had settled on the boy name for the baby while staying in the Extend-A-Stay. We were watching a sci-fi marathon, still weak and slightly flu-ish, and I suggested the name Malcolm, after the starship captain in the show *Firefly*.

"It's perfect," I declared. "Saint name, science-fiction associations, unusual enough to hang with a brother named Joaquin. It's perfect."

Ken made face at me. "If by 'perfect' you mean 'terrible.' Malcolm is a terrible name, even if he is an awesome starship captain." I sat in moody silence for a moment.

"What about Jean-Luc?" I said, half jokingly. "He was another great starship captain." Ken nodded, not immediately dismissing the idea. I tried to play it cool and kept my mouth shut.

"Well not 'Jean-Luc,'" he said thoughtfully. "No sissy French names for my sons. John-Luke." Then he snorted, "All these Catholic double-names. Mary Whatever for all the girls and John Something-or-other for the boys."

He didn't rule out the name, but it was far from settled. The biggest sticking point seemed to be whether to include a hyphen (I was strongly pro-hyphen) or omit it (Ken was anti-hyphen). For weeks we focused on the Great Hyphen Debate, the better to help us forget that we had no real idea what we were going to do when the baby finally came. The few people we had met were not ready for a 2 a.m., "Hey, can you come sleep on our couch and watch our four children so we can go to the hospital?" call, and the closest family—my aunt and uncle—were eight hours away.

My mom bought airfare to come around the due date, but there was no guarantee that I would go into labor while she was here. As I presented these problems to one of the OBs, it was agreed that they would schedule a "social induction" for the day after the due date.

We tried our hardest to avoid it, walking up and down the biking trails in town, but nothing. The day of the induction came, my mom stayed with the kids, and Ken and I went to the hospital for yet another round of Pitocin-and-waiting.

The IV was in by 9 a.m., by 4 p.m., I was only four centimeters dilated, feeling very sorry for myself.

There were three good things, though:

1. The hospital let me have all the water I wanted. I didn't have the cruel pitcher of ice chips that I would try to get to melt enough to create an actual swallow of water. Plus, there was a snack cupboard with granola bars and such that I could help myself to. Swanky!

2. The hospital had a water-birth room, and while the OB who was on duty when I delivered wouldn't let me actually deliver in the tub, it was still nice to be able to labor in the water.

3. We had the single best nurse I've ever had. She was like some cosmic apology for the nurse from Jude's birth: kind, soft-spoken, rubbed my back when I needed it and Ken needed a break. She sat next to me while I labored in pain-med-free Pitocin agony, so Ken could grab something to eat in the cafeteria. I loved her.

Finally, despite my grim skepticism, it was time to push. I pushed, and there were no explosions, no posterior babies, no giant heads, no biting of the doctor, absolutely nothing remarkable except our baby.

I once read a very angry article declaring that a fetus is nothing but a parasite. It takes everything from the host and gives nothing back in return. According to the story, people who call this "a miracle" are stupid, since it happens all the time, and everyone knows that miracles aren't common.

Shoddy science aside, I suspect the author wasn't a mother, since there is nothing that *isn't* miraculous in the birth of your child. Even the most routine, unremarkable birth is steeped in God's own mystery.

The baby was declared to be a boy, cleaned off, wrapped up, given to me, and the room cleared out. Ken and I sat in that stunned, overwhelming silence, staring at the baby and each other, completely in love with that tiny human in our arms. And then the shakes started. I suddenly felt like every bone in my body was going to break from the force of my shaking. My teeth were going to shatter and fall out of my head. I didn't feel bad, or dizzy, or nauseated; I just couldn't stop shaking. I had to give the baby to Ken; I was worried about dropping him.

Just as Ken was getting worried enough to go get a doctor, the shaking stopped. It was as if an off switch had been flipped, and my body was no longer on vibrate. We looked at each other, shrugged, and watched TV, holding the new baby and reveling in the common miracle of new life. And, probably because he was more worried about my mysterious shaking than he let on, Ken agreed to a hyphen in his fourth son's name.

The Van

When I was pregnant with Joaquin, I remember having a discussion with my friend from grade school—the one whose adorable baby was the gateway drug to my habit of childbearing. Ken and I were looking for a new car, and my friend suggested a minivan.

"They're really convenient," she said, showing me how hers had magic doors that slid open with the touch of a button. The inside of her vehicle was clean and tidy, with books, toys, and diaper paraphernalia neatly stored in a seat organizer.

It was horrifying. Unless a car has two inches of debris carpeting the floor, I don't trust it. How would you ever survive a zombie apocalypse with a car that tidy? Everyone knows that the only people in zombie movies who survive the initial outbreak are the ones who can survive off the materials safely hidden in their trashy car.

I looked at her dubiously. "I don't know. A minivan? It just screams, 'Mom.'"

She looked at me totally deadpan, then slowly lowered her eyes to my swollen abdomen straining against the fashionable maternity jeans. She then looked at some point behind my left shoulder. Following her gaze, I saw Lotus had escaped the house wearing a princess tiara, one shoe, and nothing else.

"You know what else screams, 'Mom'?" she said. "Your two-year-old."

She was right. Well, not about the clean car. I'm sticking to my guns on that one. But she was right about the futility of ever again pinning an inauthentic persona onto a car. Or anything else, really. Being a parent is exhausting. Being a parent while simultaneously pretending you aren't is just madness. So a couple of years later, when we found a used minivan at a price we could more or less afford, I knew it was the exciting first step into a new world. Also, do you know how much junk a minivan can hold? You can survive a whole bunch of zombie apocalypses with a junkmobile like that!

When we went to pick up the car at the used-car dealership, I noted with deep satisfaction that the car had a button that magically opened the side doors, just like my friend's. Lotus took one look at the gleaming white minivan and declared that it looked just like a baby beluga. At four, she was not only precocious, but also a bona fide expert in marine biology.

And so the van was christened Baby Beluga, or Baby B if you were on friendly terms with it.

Being a used van, Baby B had a little condition I like to call "possession." The "check engine" light would constantly go on, despite being fresh from a clean diagnostic check. The passenger-side window stopped working. Predictably, this happened after the window had been rolled halfway down, so Ken had to figure out a way to shimmy the glass back up. The magic button controlling the automatic side door stopped working. Of course.

But hey! It still ran, it was paid for, and it would still fit all of us, even after our third baby made an appearance. Really, as long as I kept chucking blessed salt and holy water at Baby B, things kept working. Sort of.

Baby Beluga was with us four glorious years. She carried us in junked-up splendor through Mississippi, Tennessee, Texas, Georgia, Florida, and Michigan. Also, whatever states are between Mississippi and Michigan. (I'm writing this very early in the morning and I can't be bothered to check it out for myself.)

Then, that inevitable day came when we had to bid Baby Beluga goodbye. It was our first summer in New England, where we learned with horror that Yankees do not generally build their hundred-year-old houses with central air. Now, you'd think that because we had just spent five years in the deep South, a little Connecticut summer would be nothing. You'd think we'd just laugh at it and bundle up in parkas and such. But if you'd think that, you'd be forgetting one thing that no one tells you about New England—the humidity. Like, Mississippi-levels of humidity. Maybe worse. Summer in New England feels like you are moving through a tepid bowl of clam chowder. Also, the radio stations all kept gleefully announcing that this was the hottest day of the year, with temps reaching the high 90s by noon.

Ken called me from his air-conditioned day spa known as "work," and told me to load the kids into Baby B, head over the mountain, and go to Cabela's.

"There'll be air-conditioning, the kids can look at all the dead animals, and you can look at camping gear." I tell you, that man is a keeper. And brilliant.

His suggestion was so attractive that it was worth hunting down clothes, shoes, and socks for five tiny humans, loading them into the van, buckling them up, and heading over the mountain on the hottest day of the year.

I had turned Baby B's air conditioning on full blast. After about ten minutes, a blissful hush fell over the van as six human beings took their first non-waterlogged breaths all day. It was glorious. The swampy sheen of moisture that had coated us evaporated. As I began the ascent of the mountain, I sang along happily with the song on the radio and daydreamed about sub-zero sleeping bags.

Then, about three hundred yards from the top of the mountain, Baby B shuffled loose the mortal coil. She just stopped. I couldn't accelerate, because the engine was dead. I could break and coast, and so I sort of drifted onto the shoulder of Avon Mountain. At rush hour.

I sat there for a moment, trying to figure out what to do, while four of the five kids, who had been lulled into sleep by the air-conditioning, started angrily waking up as the humidity crept back into the air.

I didn't have a cell phone, because I live a secret life as an Amish person. I usually enjoyed a feeling of smug superiority when people would incredulously ask how I was brave enough to set foot outside my house with five children and no phone. But at this particular moment, I was not feeling smug, but very, very stupid.

There was a line of traffic rapidly forming as people tried to maneuver past my minivan, which was not actually parked as neatly on the shoulder as I had imagined. I flagged down the first driver who was foolish enough to establish eye contact with me, and he grudgingly pulled over, let me borrow his cell phone, and pushed my van all the way off the road. He sighed wearily and fled back to his car after I thanked him, probably cursing himself for breaking that most primal of New England social codes — do not make eye contact with strangers.

Eventually, a police officer came, directed traffic, and let me use his cell phone to call a tow truck while I waited for Ken to come get us. I went back into the van to check on the kids. Most of them needed to pee, so I gave each of them one of the half-dozen Burger King cups littering the floor (see? handy!) and surreptitiously dumped the contents behind Baby B while the cop wasn't looking.

Hours later, we were all back at our (non-air-conditioned) home, an unfixable Baby B had been towed down our driveway, and I moodily realized I hadn't even gotten to check out camping gear. Even worse, we needed to find another van.

Ken and I checked out the used-car websites, where we had a brief, pride-fueled argument about what type of car we should be looking for. I was perfectly happy with another minivan. Or, barring that, one of those SUV things that I had seen all over the place in Connecticut. Mostly, the people driving SUVs were very thin, waifish women, so I thought driving one of those things must be a surefire weight-loss plan.

Ken, however, was firmly in the Full-Size Passenger Van camp. You know the ones I'm talking about. The ones that are primarily used as shuttles for churches with names like Apostolic Holy Fire Church of Jesus in God of Prophecy and the people seated within look vaguely like the characters from *Children of the Corn*. If the Full-Size Passenger Van wasn't schlepping

Malachi and Obadiah to and from revivals, it was used as a prison van. Neither scenario was something I wanted people to associate with my family. Ultimately, though, Ken's good sense won out. Five kids already, and who knew how many more to come? A good passenger van is built like a tank and really can last forever. And, despite the fact that Ken told me I absolutely could not get an airbrushed mural of Our Lady of Guadalupe riding a unicorn over a sparkling river on the side of the new van, I eventually found myself perversely excited about getting a full-size van.

Do you know how much zombie-fighting junk you can store on the floor of one of those suckers?

10

∽

The Champions

Armed with a sense of zeal and a giant-size van to cart us in, we were all fired up to go evangelize this strange new culture we found ourselves in. We were going to bring the light of Christ to a dark and stormy New England—like missionaries, bravely preaching in hostile lands, only with less of a threat of cannibalism.

What better way to make ourselves accessible to our new neighbors than by getting pregnant with our sixth child? Sure, sure, my fifth pregnancy was met with near-universal horror, but maybe this time around, the tipping point would have been reached and this baby would be a sort of Ambassador of Love and Life.

Hope springs eternal, right?

Interestingly, the sixth pregnancy didn't seem to inspire the same hostility as the previous one. I don't know if it was that my perception had been mellowed or if people just pegged me for crazy and therefore left me alone, but I didn't have the same angry comments lobbed at me as I had previously.

I took that as a major victory for the Kingdom.

This time, instead of people asking me if we (always "we," as in both of us, just to be safe) were going to "get fixed," the favorite question was "What are you going to do if it's another boy?"

At first I was puzzled by this question. What did they *think* I was going to do? Finally crack, and run screaming for the hills—the fifth son being the straw that broke my back? Then I realized they were asking about logistics—in a four-bedroom house, how were sleeping arrangements going to be worked out with such a boy-heavy population?

I took it as another victory that people's primary concern was now bunk beds and mattresses, rather than a speedy sterilization of my husband and me.

The due date came and went, as it always does. My parents made the fourteen-hour trip from Michigan to Connecticut to help with a baby who, despite such drastic measures as a four-mile hike up and back down a mountain and the ingestion of copious amounts of Indian food, refused to show up. I agreed to have my membranes stripped, which the doctor couldn't even do, since the baby was still so high up in my abdominal cavity. A week passed. My parents left. I wept and fasted, wept and prayed. Still no baby.

An induction was scheduled for precisely twenty-eight hours after my parents left for home, and my next-door neighbor and her mother agreed to watch the kids for us so Ken could be there for the birth.

The day before the induction, I was what the kids like to call "a hot mess." I was convinced I was going to die in childbirth. I was convinced the baby was going to have some birth defect that would result in unbearable, insurmountable stress put upon the family. I spent most of Sunday on the edge of tears, watching my children with uncomfortable intensity, trying to burn in my mind forever the images of what were surely our last moments together. I made a Sunday dinner that verged on gluttonous, convinced this was the last time I would ever cook for my people. I begged God to spare me. I begged anyone who had the misfortune of asking me how I was doing to offer up Rosaries, novenas, Holy Hours, whatever, for me.

See? Hot mess.

Finally, I asked God to do one of two things for me—if all this hysteria was the result of a spiritual attack, to shelter me from it, since I was clearly not ready to face a challenge of this magnitude. If it wasn't a spiritual attack, but a forewarning of things to come, then I begged for the grace to face it with internal peace and joy.

Then I told Ken about my worries, got soundly teased for them, and managed to fall asleep.

God, I love that man.

I woke up before my alarm Monday morning, took a shower, spent some time trying to figure out how much makeup would cross that line between "well groomed" and "wildly inappropriate for impending labor and childbirth." (Final decision: foundation, blush, eyeliner. No eyeshadow, mascara, or lipstick. Hair blow-dried, but not curled. When I'm nervous, I like to overthink things.)

My neighbor's mother came. I went over what is probably the only schedule my children have ever been on. I'm not kidding. Their day was scripted in half-hour segments, menus for each meal included, ingredients laid out on the kitchen island, the whole nine yards. I was exhausted just looking at it.

I hugged them all goodbye and assured them that this time the doctor's appointment would result in a new sibling. Joaquin, Gabriel, and John-Luke were fine with me leaving, so weary were they of doctor's appointments that didn't produce a baby.

Lotus and Jude howled. I have a gold locket that my grandfather gave me when I was two, and ever since Joaquin's birth, I've let Lotus wear the locket the whole time I'm in the hospital for a new baby. Wearing this mollified her somewhat, but Jude was inconsolable. I left him crying in front of the TV while I got in the car, feeling guilty and morose and irritated with the whole stupid birthing thing.

We got to the hospital, parked, checked in, and were introduced to our labor and delivery nurse.

Her name was Lorraine, she was Irish, and she spent a good portion of her time running off assorted interns who kept inexplicably showing up at my bedside to perform unnecessary internal exams on me. One of them, who was doubting my ability to deliver what he was estimating to be an eight-pound baby, she actually ushered out into the hall and read him the riot act.

From my bed, I could hear the phrase "proven pelvis" being thrown around a lot. I loved her.

Even my doctor was strangely deferential to her, asking Nurse Lorraine's opinion on what induction technique to attempt. In fact, the only flaw I could find in Nurse Lorraine was her repeated comparison of my uterus to a "stretched-out pair of underwear."

Bear with me here. Stop reading for a moment, and get a proper Irish brogue good and clear in your head.

Got it? Okay, now, in that accent (the more outrageous, the better), read the following: "Well, the reason you haven't gone into labor on your own, dear, is because this is your sixth child. Your uterus is like a pair of underwear. When it's good and new, it's very stretchy, lots of strength in that elastic. But as it gets used, as it gets older and stretched out one too many times, it loses its elasticity. That's what your uterus is like. You've just stretched it out so many times that it can't get that baby out on its own."

Accurate medical description or no, you have to admit that hearing a body part likened to a pair of grubby underpants is astounding. Hearing it likened to a pair of grubby underpants by someone with an Irish accent is hypnotic.

In the end, the good doctor and the excellent nurse decided to give me a dose of a something *before* starting the hated, painful Pitocin drip.

Fine. I kept eyeballing that bag of Pitocin balefully, hating it, and wishing I could set it on fire with sheer force of will. Failing that, I alternated between reading chapters of *Hunger Games* and sending out obnoxious Tweets. I had no problem sharing my laborious, stretched-out-underpants misery with social media.

I could feel contractions, rhythmic ones, even, but I figured the Pitocin would be started any moment now. I'd be begging for painkillers within the hour.

Then Nurse Lorraine told me my contractions were at the point where Pitocin couldn't be started, since I was now officially in active labor, and it was like the heavens opened, and fat little cherubs came out to frolic and sing songs. No Pitocin! Labor had started!

The doctor materialized out of nowhere while I was eating an orange Popsicle Lorraine had brought me. Lorraine ran the doctor off until I had finished my Popsicle.

Once I was done with my first caloric intake in eighteen hours, the doctor checked my progress. I was now five to six centimeters dilated and 90 percent effaced. She asked me if I minded her breaking my waters. I said, "Hell no, let's get this show on the road!" So my waters were broken, and that's when the first hiccup of the labor was discovered.

The amniotic fluid had meconium in it (for those of you who are visually minded, think: the most disgusting split pea soup you've ever seen), so now a pediatrician from the NICU had to be present at the birth in case the baby ended up inhaling any of it during delivery. My doctor explained that I would need to stop all pushing once the head was delivered so she could suction out the nose and throat to see if the fluid was clear, or if there was meconium present. All clear would mean all was well; meconium in the fluid would mean immediate NICU for the baby to treat for meconium aspiration.

As I listened to the doctor explain all this, a part of me marveled at my response. Whereas with Lotus, in my pre-Christian days, I firmly thought that everything my child needed were things I could provide through sheer force of will, now, ten years and a conversion later, I saw things from a radically different perspective. Now I realized that I am utterly dependent on God's grace, protection, and love. Now I realized that a child was one of greatest blessings God would ever give me, and as such, the child was not a prop to bend to my will. I couldn't force this baby to have clear lungs upon birth. And that was okay, because I could ask God to protect us. I could pray.

So I started praying. I was vividly aware of all the people I knew, people who loved me, Ken, and our family, who were praying for us right at that very moment. In the days before the induction, I had gotten e-mails and phone calls from people all over the world telling me they would be covering the whole delivery process in prayer, so at that moment, we prayed together.

I think it is a comment on the transcendent nature of God when I say that there were prayers coming from all parts of the globe during labor. And I think it's a comment on the power of prayer when I say that when I got the news of this possibly serious development, I was absolutely calm. I knew God had us in the palm of His hand. I floated on all those prayers from six centimeters, to eight centimeters, to a shot of Nubain, to nine and a half centimeters and was sure that it wasn't time to push since the NICU pediatrician needed to be called in.

Awesome Lorraine's shift had ended a few moments before, and we were now stuck with a very bad, possibly crazy, new nurse. Ken told our new nurse to just leave me alone—I would let everyone know when it was time to push.

I kept floating on those prayers and marveled that for the first time, I was able to observe each contraction as pressure, and not precisely pain. I floated on them when I felt the first need to push, and the room swirled into carefully controlled action. The prayers carried the baby down the birth canal in one push. They filled the room as the second push delivered the head. The prayers were already ringing out in thanksgiving as all the fluid suctioned out of the baby's nose and mouth came back clear.

And when that final push delivered the rest of the baby into the world, and I could hear Ken's voice saying, "I'm no doctor, but I think it's a girl," my gasping Hail Mary joined all the prayers already with us.

A girl! Our first girl in ten years. Beautiful, healthy, wonderful, seven-pound, eleven-ounce Veronica Rosemary, who was born on St. Rose Venerini's feast day.

But the prayers didn't stop there. They were already on the job for us when blood work revealed that Veronica and I had exchanged our incompatible blood during delivery, and she tested Coombs positive. All those prayers whispered to her little body when her twenty-four-hour bilirubin levels were still elevated. And by the time she was retested eighteen hours later, she was fine.

So there we were, now a family of eight. I didn't die. The baby was fine. As the old saying goes, "A baby is born with a loaf of bread under each arm," and the bread this one brought was spiritual bread, feeding that part of me that was starving for a reminder of the power of prayer.

We Are the Champions

Spiritual bread aside, at some point Ken returned to work, and I had to figure out how to procure us physical bread. Which meant a trip to the grocery store.

No matter how many children you have, those first outings are always a shock. One more person to get ready. One more car seat to buckle up. One more head to count in an attempt never to bring the movie *Home Alone* to real life. I'd put it off long enough; a trip to the grocery store was essential. And, given Ken's hours, it meant that the trip would involve me and my entire six-child entourage.

"We Are the Champions" was playing when I started the van. And not the last few bars—the start of the song! I took this as an auspicious sign and giddily belted it out with Freddy Mercury while the final car-seat adjustments were made. I did a quick head count: six kids, clothed, shod, buckled in their seats and gleefully singing along with Freddy and me.

The very stars themselves had aligned to make this a most prodigious start to grocery shopping—an event I usually looked forward to as I would a plague outbreak.

The store was less than three miles up the road, so the song had barely ended when we pulled into a parking space. The

The Champions

four-year-old was still singing, bobbing his head and declaring to the assembled siblings in the van that he was, in fact, a champion. I strapped the baby onto my back in her sling and looked for a cart.

I encountered the first road bump when I realized that in the entire parking lot, the only cart available was the dreaded kiddie-car cart.

I loathe the car cart. It is the bête noire of my domestic existence. It's impossible to steer, and it causes my children to have delusions of grandeur, imagining that they're policemen chasing down bad guys, complete with self-provided sirens. Also not helpful is the fact that the car cart puts little hands at the perfect level to sweep across the lowest shelves, knocking three dozen cans of soup into the aisle in an instant.

My moment of indecision cost me, and all the kids spilled out of the van, spotted the car cart, and began arguing over who would get to ride in it.

There were seven of us standing there in the gusty winds of that late April day. Six of us were under the age of eleven. More than half of us were wearing superhero costumes of some sort, and various capes fluttered dramatically in the breeze. Three of our group were about to start brawling right there next to the cart return over who got to pretend-steer a yellow plastic car.

We were, in fact, the champions.

I double-checked to make sure I had the list, arbitrarily selected two kids for car privileges, distracted the howling odd-man-out with some stale goldfish crackers found lurking in the bottom of my purse, and off we went, like some carnival troupe that just rolled into town.

We made it as far as the produce section before being stopped by the first spectator.

"Wow! Just … wow!" The woman was in her mid-forties and had nothing but organic merchandise in her cart. I noticed this because she had parked her cart directly in front of mine, cutting off all obvious escape routes. The boys, from their car perch, leaned forward and started poking her groceries.

"Are they all yours?" I smiled and nodded. I felt, rather than saw, my oldest child tense up at the words and slink behind me. Lotus was toeing the threshold of adolescence, that place where attention is simultaneously craved and despised. The Family-Size Litany was attention she preferred to avoid.

The woman stared at the kids, as if she had never seen children before. She didn't say anything else, but didn't move her cart, either. It was hard not to feel like some exotic insect she had trapped in a jar. The moment stretched on uncomfortably.

Finally, the boys decided to take matters into their own hands. Grabbing hold of the woman's cart, they moved it to the right, crashing it into her ankle and bringing the whole interaction to a quick end.

I didn't even correct them for that. Organic Foodstuffs sort of had it coming.

I awkwardly shoved the behemoth cart through the aisles, leaving the wreckage of my horrible steering and the boys' gleeful grabbing in my wake. The kids old enough not to be strapped in a cart or sling followed behind, picking up cans and cartons and bags of potatoes while laughing at my poor steering skills.

We were a finely oiled, grocery-shopping machine. Items were placed in the cart with skillful precision, the list divided into sections, and anyone old enough to feel uncomfortable wearing a superhero costume in public was given a set of things to find. All went well—Freddy Mercury levels of well—until we approached the dairy case.

The Champions

There we found our progress blocked by a man roughly fifty years old, who actually stood in the middle of our path, with arms slightly raised from his sides, as if he were going to restrain us physically if we tried to pass him. His mouth was wide open in disbelief; I saw his glassy, bloodshot eyes sweep over all my kids, nodding his head as he counted them up.

I looked him full in the face, expectantly. I tried to move my cart to the left of him, and he shifted his body to block me. I tried to move to his right but was blocked again. It was like a scene from *Gunfight at the O.K. Corral*. I expected a tumbleweed to blow past.

"Excuse me. I'd like to get by." I allowed the tiniest bit of irritation to seep into my voice.

The man blinked, as if he were coming out of a trance, and shuffled *just* enough to one side so we could pass him.

The little boys grabbed his pant leg as we passed.

At that point, it was only the case of beer in the cart that kept me from terminating the whole horrible process right there and walking out of the store, leaving a full load of groceries in my wake.

Then we met *her*. She was an elderly lady wearing a lavender skirt and matching blazer. Her hair was in a fat, flat bun on top of her head, and steely gray wisps of it had come loose to brush her shoulders. I had passed her twice already, and both times she kept looking at us out of the corner of her eye. The third time our paths crossed, she spoke.

"Are they all yours?" I smiled and nodded, once again, feeling like a marionette. I felt Lotus skulk back to her hiding spot behind me. The old lady smiled back. "I had five. Five in the first ten years of marriage."

Now my smile was genuine.

"We've got six in twelve!" We were like two battle-tested generals, swapping war stories. She nodded and looked at each kid, smiling right into their eyes. There was no feeling of being some exotic specimen with this woman. With her the sense of nostalgia was palpable and friendly. I felt my shoulders relax, and my daughter half-peered out from around me. We'd discovered a little oasis in the international-food aisle.

Cue little boys in the car, cue three dozen soup cans spilling into the isle. Cue frazzled stock clerk, who had been trailing us at a discreet distance. The lady said her goodbyes, and we stocked up on the Pope John Paul II candles that were stacked neatly next to the tortillas and headed to the checkout. From there, the parking lot, the van, and finally home.

And all of us were singing "We Are the Champions" softly under our breaths.

Raising Pope Awesome and His Posse of Saints

I woke up with a sinus infection. I could tell just by the way my head felt. The kind of pain that in my pre-mothering days would have merited a call into work and a well-deserved sick day. But those days were long gone, and there were no sick days. Plus, this was Pope Benedict's final day as Pontiff, and I couldn't let him go without watching him leave.

I knew that watching Benedict leave the Vatican for the last time as Pope was going to be physically painful for me. Oh sure, emotional pain in the form of a bittersweet goodbye, but even worse—physical pain as a result of my sinus cavities filling up to bursting as I cried those odd, confusing tears.

But this was a once-in-a-lifetime sort of thing. Papal abdications don't happen every day, and I felt that my homeschool card would be revoked if I didn't have my kids watch history unfold.

The Champions

I called them all in front of the computer to watch EWTN's live streaming of the events. Four-year-old Jude sat in my lap and surveyed the scene with a creased brow and serious expression. "What's this, Mama?" he asked suspiciously. I explained that we were watching the current Pope leave the Vatican for the last time. Jude was silent for a moment, watching closely.

"Who's the next Pope?" he asked after a while.

"I don't know. No one but God knows."

Jude turned around to look at me. "Well then," he said, "I'll do it. I'll be the next Pope." I smiled a little at the boy. This was coming from the child who cannot get through Mass without taking a nap on the pew or demanding that he get a piece "of that cracker."

Yes, we've had multiple discussions about how it's not a "cracker"—it's Jesus. But things take a while to sink in with The Jude sometimes. Pope Jude. I snorted a bit to myself. But he didn't let the idea go.

"Who are those people?" he demanded, stabbing a finger at the image of a brightly costumed soldier on the computer screen.

"That's a member of the Swiss Guard. They're like super-special soldiers who are there to guard the Pope."

"Like a police officer?"

"Sort of. But while a police officer is there to help everyone, the Swiss Guard is there only for the Pope."

"An army guy? The Pope gets his own army guys?" Jude was now pressing his face right against the screen, resulting in two brothers shoving him aside so they could see.

Next to me, Lotus sighed heavily. I glanced over at her.

"I suppose only men can be Swiss Guards, too," she muttered. As the oldest child, she has never been okay about being told she can't accomplish something, and male-only jobs irritate her.

"Yup," I said. "Only men. And only Swiss men. And only un-married Swiss men. And only unmarried Swiss men between nineteen and thirty years old who are at least five feet, eight inches tall."

Her eyes widened at the requirements, then settled into a satisfied glow. If she couldn't be a Swiss Guard, she was happy knowing that the majority of the world couldn't be one either.

Jude, however, cared only about the Swiss Guard in relation to his upcoming papal appointment.

"They're cool," he announced. "I'll take them."

We watched a few more moments in silence. Then Jude spoke again. "Mama? When I'm Pope, will I be rich?"

I tried to explain that the Pope has no personal possessions of his own, but that he doesn't really need money, since the Church meets his needs.

"So people just *give* him things that he wants?" Jude has a way of forcing you into a black-and-white answer.

"More or less," I said hesitantly.

"When I'm Pope, and I don't have money, who will give me new video games? The Swiss Guards? I bet they will. If they don't, I'll punch them in the face."

There was an audible gasp from three of the children. The thought of a Pope punching anyone in the face, let alone a Swiss Guard over a video game, was too much for them. They all started shouting at Jude. Unperturbed, he raised both arms, and made a "settle down" gesture. Amusingly, his siblings did, in fact, settle down.

A few more silent moments passed. Then, on the screen, a door opened. Out came Benedict, dressed all in white, carrying a cane and walking slowly—so, so slowly. I teared up, and my head began to pound from the increased pressure.

Jude turned to look at me, alarmed by my sniffling. "Is that the Pope?" he asked. I nodded yes, not trusting myself to speak. "Where does he live?"

With a voice thick with tears, I gave a brief explanation of the Vatican and Castel Gandolfo, which could be seen on the screen.

Jude surveyed it briefly, then nodded again. "That's cool. I like it. I'll live there, and you can stay with me forever and ever, Mama."

I smiled and blew my nose. Jude continued. "When I'm Pope, I'll marry you."

"You can't be married when you're Pope, honey," I said.

"Why not?"

"Because the Pope is a priest. And priests don't get married." He stared at me for a long moment and then turned back to the screen. Benedict was walking along the hallway, out into the courtyard and was bid farewell by various cardinals.

"Hey, Jude. When you're Pope, what will your name be?" asked the seven-year-old, who is already careful to call things by their correct name.

Jude sniffed imperiously. "I'll be Saint Jude."

"You can't be that. You have to have a papal name." Joaquin explained. Then he had a thought: "Oh! How about Pope Awesome the First?"

The kids all decided that Pope Awesome the First was a fine name indeed, and silence fell over us again.

We watched the Holy Father board a helicopter, which earned Jude's approval, then be lifted off into the air, as all the bells of St. Peter's sounded out. I blew my nose again and felt my heart get very sad. It lasted only a moment, however, before Jude was at it again.

"Can I be Pope when I'm four?" I shook my head no. He thought for a second. "Then I'll wait until I'm ten." His siblings were all too engrossed in the news coverage to correct him.

"Mama? Where is the Pope place?" he asked.

"In Rome, baby."

"Is that far? Can I walk there?" He glanced at the world map tacked up on the wall.

I smiled. "Nope. It's too far to walk there."

He was not deterred. "Then drop me off at my Pope place, okay, Mama? Then you can introduce me as Pope Awesome the First to my soldiers."

"But you're not Pope, honey." I sensed that it might be time to remind Jude of this small fact, just to head off bigger problems down the road.

"Yes, I am! I am Pope. That other guy left. We need a Pope. I'll do it."

"You have to be elected by the College of Cardinals first, sweetie."

"Oh," he said, stopping for only a split second. "Well, they did that. Now drop me off at my Pope place."

With this, he slid off my lap, grabbed his sneakers, and started putting them on. He looked up at his sister. "And Lotus, when I'm Pope, you can come into my office whenever you want. I promise. Oh … wait. Mama, does the Pope have an office?"

So there, in my homeschool classroom, the 266th Pope was self-elected.

Pope Awesome the First, humble servant of God.

Spurred on by some unknown, unspoken cue, all the other children pulled themselves away from the computer and got their shoes on, too. The big kids helped the little kids get ready,

The Champions

and before I knew it, they'd all filed out of the schoolroom, up the stairs, and out to the van, buckling themselves into their car seats and waiting expectantly for me to take them—well, *somewhere*, I guess. I suppose it didn't matter where, really.

Bemused and chuckling softly, I followed them, passing Ken in the process. He watched the line of children file past him, then looked at me quizzically. "Where are we going?" he asked, and all I could do was answer with a shrug. The two of us walked to the van, got in, and I looked at the faces of my children. Pope Awesome and his posse of saints looked back at me happily; six inscrutable blessings showered upon me by a merciful and loving God. And next to me, their father, the love of my life, who had been by my side almost as long as God had been.

Ken put the key in the ignition and backed Big B out of the driveway. I had no idea where we were going. But I knew it would be better than anything we could have planned in our wildest dreams.

∞

Acknowledgments

Here is where I thank a bunch of people because it's my book, and I do what I like. Technically, the book's over, but if you're one of those weirdos who likes to stay until the end of the credits at a movie, then chances are you'll like this page.

Mom and Dad and Ian — thank you for giving me the best childhood anyone could want. The only thing that was missing was a pony, but since I think I turned out okay, I guess not giving me a pony was for the best.

Dave and Melanie — thank you for getting married, having Ken, and moving to Michigan so I could take him off your hands. Debra, I already thanked you earlier in the book, so you can skip the rest of this.

Kim — thank you for always keeping a place for me at your table. Even if I have to shove a kid out of his seat for it.

Many, many thanks to **Dwija, Jessica, and Mary Kate**, who endured countless texts and emails demanding to know things like, "How many poison control stories do you think I can include before someone calls CPS?" or "If I go a whole chapter without mentioning poop, will people think I've sold out?"

Thank you to **Eric**, who read the whole first draft of this book while on vacation and even had nice things to say about it.

Acknowledgments

Charlie at Sophia Institute Press, who took a chance on this book when no one else would, and **Duncan**, who suggested I write a different book from the proposed one—thank you both from the bottom of my heart.

Lotus, Joaquin, Gabriel, Jude, John-Luke, and Veronica—thank you for being so patient all those times you wanted me to do something like cook you dinner or give you a bath but I told you to hang on a second because I was writing. Good news: second's up. Bad news: we're having broccoli for dinner.

And **Ken**—thank you for being patient with me when this book made me insane. Thank you for pretending the insanity was because of this book. Thank you for making me your wife, and thank you for encouraging me to become so awesome at it.

Lastly, thank **you**, (*please state your name here*), for spending hard-earned money and free time reading this book. I hope it made you think about God and His love and maybe gave you a couple of laughs along the way.

Parts of this book were originally published on **catholicexchange.com** *and* **aleteia.org**.

∽

About the Author

As a small girl, Cari Donaldson wanted to be a vegetarian, a veterinarian, and an author. Once she realized how much math was involved in being a vet, she scrapped that idea. Being a vegetarian and writing this book involved almost no math, however, so she was able to accomplish them both. She now lives in Connecticut with her husband, six children, twenty chickens, and one dog. When her many overlords allow it, she details her family life at www.clan-donaldson.com.

An Invitation

Reader, the book that you hold in your hands was published by Sophia Institute Press. Sophia Institute seeks to to nurture the spiritual, moral, and cultural life of souls and to spread the Gospel of Christ in conformity with the authentic teachings of the Roman Catholic Church. Our press fulfills this mission by offering translations, reprints, and new publications that afford readers a rich source of the enduring wisdom of mankind.

We also operate two popular online Catholic resources: CrisisMagazine.com and CatholicExchange.com.

Crisis Magazine provides insightful cultural analysis that arms readers with the arguments necessary for navigating the ideological and theological minefields of the day. *Catholic Exchange* provides world news from a Catholic perspective as well as daily devotionals and articles that will help you to grow in holiness and live a life consistent with the teachings of the Church.

Sophia Institute Press also serves as the publisher for the Thomas More College of Liberal Arts and Holy Spirit College. Both colleges provide university-level education under the guiding light of Catholic teaching. If you know a young person seeking a college that takes seriously the adventure of learning and the quest for truth, please bring these institutions to his attention.

www.SophiaInstitute.com
www.CatholicExchange.com
www.CrisisMagazine.com

Sophia Institute Press® is a registered trademark of Sophia Institute. Sophia Institute is a tax-exempt institution as defined by the Internal Revenue Code, Section 501(c)(3). Tax I.D. 22-2548708.